BIDDING
A BRIDGE HAND

(formerly titled: *Develop Your Bidding Judgment*)

by
TERENCE REESE

DOVER PUBLICATIONS, INC.
NEW YORK

Published in Canada by General Publishing Company, Ltd., 30 Lesmill Road, Don Mills, Toronto, Ontario.
Published in the United Kingdom by Constable and Company, Ltd., 10 Orange Street, London WC 2.

This Dover edition, first published in 1972, is an unabridged and unaltered republication of the work originally published in 1962 by Sterling Publishing Company, Inc., under the title *Develop Your Bidding Judgment*. It is reprinted by special arrangement with Sterling Publishing Company, Inc., 419 Park Avenue South, New York, New York 10016.

International Standard Book Number: 0-486-22830-4
Library of Congress Catalog Card Number: 73-188817

Manufactured in the United States of America
Dover Publications, Inc.
180 Varick Street
New York, N.Y. 10014

CONTENTS

Foreword

Most players, in these days, have evolved a reasonable technique of constructive bidding which serves them for 75 per cent of all deals. In this book I aim to deal with the remaining 25 per cent where a player is out on his own and must use his judgment—where no text-book or point count will help him, and where bidding system has little bearing.

I have followed the over-the-shoulder technique which seemed popular in *Play Bridge with Reese*. The reader shares my thoughts at every stage of the bidding. Whether he agrees with my eventual answer is not so important—naturally there may be differences in bidding style that will affect the decision. The test is: Has some train of thought, some general principle, emerged from the discussion which will perhaps help to solve a later problem at the table?

The setting of the problems is given sometimes as rubber bridge, sometimes as a team event with international match-point scoring, sometimes as a match-pointed pairs tournament. The objectives at IMP scoring are broadly similar to those at rubber bridge. In a pairs event the bidding is keener in the sense that a player must strive to gain small advantages even at the risk of an occasional disaster.

It is assumed throughout that partner is a good player. True, one needs judgment to play with bad partners also, but what is right with one bad partner is apt to be wrong with another, so that general principles cannot be usefully extracted.

The competition pages of the bridge magazines are a standard source for good problems. I have derived many ideas from the *Bridge World's* Masters Solvers' Club, directed by Albert Morehead and Alphonse Moyse, Jr., and still more from the *British Bridge World* feature, One Hundred Up. I am especially indebted to successive editors, Albert Dormer and Alan Truscott, and to such veteran panelists as Peter

Swinnerton-Dyer, Edmund Phillips, Bob and Jim Sharples, Herman Filarski and others, whose comments I have been able to study and whose opinions I have often anonymously quoted—sometimes, *il faut l'admettre*, in a contrary sense!

This book is destined to appear in both British and American editions. To avoid an excessive number of changes, there has been compromise in respect of a few common words. Thus British readers are asked to accept 'honor,' American readers 'defence.'

Terence Reese

There is a demand nowadays for the
man who can make wrong appear right.
—Publius Terentius Afer (190-159 B.C.)

A Note on Bidding the Opponent's Suit

I have tried, in the problems that follow, to steer clear of special conventions, but a word may be helpful about the use of a bid in the opponent's suit. This used to promise considerable strength and in principle it confirmed partner's suit as trump. The modern style is to treat it as a general-purpose force, for use whenever the best denomination is in doubt.

Suppose that the bidding goes:

South	West	North	East
1♣	1♡	1♠	Pass
2♡			

South may make this bid of Two Hearts for any one of the following reasons:

(*a*) To show excellent support for spades. This is the traditional use of the bid, and South's intentions will become clear when he supports spades on a later round.

(*b*) To see if partner possesses a guard in hearts and can bid no trump. When used for this purpose, the bid has the technical name in Britain of the Directional Asking Bid, in America of the West Coast Cue-Bid.

(*c*) In a general way, to ask partner to describe his hand further—for example, by supporting clubs or rebidding his spades.

It will be noted that the bid does not promise any special holding in the opponent's suit. The frequency with which it crops up in this text is proof, I think, of its value in the sense described.

PART ONE

Problems in Constructive Bidding

The sequence of hands in this book is not especially significant. Many could have been classified under more than one heading, and there is no reason why the reader should not dip in where he pleases.

The method of studying each individual problem could be important. My suggestion is that after noting the list of alternatives you think out the problem and, for choice, write down how you would mark the various calls. If, when you read on, you disagree with my answer and are not impressed by the argument, come back to the example in a week's time and see if it strikes you at all differently.

In this first group of questions the opponents may in some cases have entered the bidding, but the eventual decisions are not competitive. The problem is to find the best answer in a constructive sequence.

° 1. Look in the Mirror

In a team event, with neither side vulnerable, I hold as dealer:

♠ K Q 9 8   ♡ A K 10 5 2   ◇ 4   ♣ A 5 2

The hand is worth a reverse by my methods, so I make the natural opening of **One Heart.** My partner responds **Two Diamonds** and I bid **Two Spades,** as planned. Now partner jumps to **Four Diamonds.** I have to find a suitable call after the sequence:

South	West	North	East
1♡	Pass	2◇	Pass
2♠	Pass	4◇	Pass
?			

The Alternatives

Depending on how I assess the prospects of game or slam, I can pass, raise to Five Diamonds, or make a more aggressive call such as 4NT or Five Clubs. I can also repeat my hearts. That seems to cover the field:

Five Diamonds
Five Clubs
4NT
Four Hearts
Pass

The Choice

There are two ways of approaching a decision of this kind in a constructive sequence. One is to form an estimate of partner's hand, put the two together, and so try to judge the final contract. The other is to concentrate mainly on one's own holding and determine whether one has something in reserve.

At various points in this book I construct possible hands for partner, but I want to establish at the start that the first step always should be to study one's own resources. Having decided whether you have anything more to show, you can next ask yourself whether your reserve strength seems to fit in well with what you imagine partner to hold.

Taking things in their proper order, then, how much money have I left in my pocket, as it were, after opening One Heart and reversing with Two Spades? Obviously very little. If my Ace of clubs had been the King I would merely have bid 2NT on the second round.

Next, has partner's bidding improved my hand in any way? No, indeed! He has persisted in calling my singleton. He hasn't mentioned clubs or shown any sign that he can fill in my hearts.

It follows that my next call should be of a minimum nature. Should I pass? No, that would go too far. Partner has responded at the level of Two and made a jump as well. There should be a sound play for game at some contract. Moreover, partner will not be expecting me to pass in a sequence where both players have made encouraging bids. Nor will he want me to pass, for he will be at least as strong as:

(1) ♠ A x   ♡ x x   ◇ K Q J 9 x x   ♣ x x x

He might also be stronger and have his eye on a slam. This is another possible hand:

(2) ♠ A x x   ♡ J x   ◇ A K 10 x x x   ♣ Q x

4NT and Five Clubs

It would be wrong to pass in my position and equally wrong to make any slam suggestion. Whether 4NT would be natural or conventional in this sequence is a matter for partnership agreement, but it would be ill-judged in either sense. If natural, it would probably be the wrong contract, and if conventional it would be useless, for the slam is going to depend not on Aces but on the solidity of the suits.

Five Clubs would be a slam try in diamonds, for I would not be trying to find a fit in a new suit at this level. It would be right if I had, say, J x in diamonds and A x in clubs, but on the present hand it would be too ambitious.

Four Hearts and Five Diamonds

We are left with the two calls that give least encouragement, Four Hearts and a raise of diamonds. Since I have already shown five hearts by implication, it would give an exaggerated impression of their

13

strength to bid them again. With hand (1) above, partner would give up and we would be in a very poor contract.

To raise to Five Diamonds on a singleton is not ideal, but partner, to by-pass 3NT, must either have good diamonds, as in example (1), or a generally good hand as in (2). With hand (2) we would be safer in 3NT or Four Hearts, but we have passed beyond 3NT and if I bid Four Hearts we shall not stop there. True, over Five Diamonds he might go to Six, but he should reckon to lose either a diamond and a club, or two clubs, or their equivalent.

Whatever its disadvantages, the fact is that no call other than Five Diamonds makes the slightest appeal. A pass would at any rate result in a plus score and one might emerge safely from Five Clubs, so I mark the alternatives:

Five Diamonds	10
Five Clubs	4
Pass	4
Four Hearts	3
4NT	2

Reflections on the Bidding

It was not necessary here for South to begin constructing possible hands for his partner. South knew that he had nothing in reserve and he had to choose the most likely game spot.

When a situation of this sort turns up in rubber bridge, players tend automatically to bid Four Hearts, in the manner of raconteurs who tell the same indifferent story many times over.

2. Long Memory

At rubber bridge, with our side vulnerable, I pick up a hand well outside my normal range in this form of contest:

♠ K 2 ♡ A K 7 6 5 ◇ A K 6 ♣ A K 7

East deals and passes and I open **Two Clubs,** the big bid in our system. West passes and North bids **Two Diamonds,** the negative response. East **doubles** this, presumably on the strength of a diamond suit. I have three possible calls now. I could pass to see what my partner would say, I could bid 2NT, defining my general strength, or I could show my hearts. I was going to bid **Two Hearts** if East had not doubled Two Diamonds, and that seems the straightforward action now.

West introduces **Three Clubs** (with diamond support in reserve, I dare say), partner bids **Three Spades,** and East passes. The bidding so far:

South	West	North	East
—	—	—	Pass
2♣	Pass	2◇	Double
2♡	3♣	3♠	Pass
?			

It is a close decision now between Four Spades and 3NT. If partner has something like Q J 9 x x in spades with no sure entry we may be better off in the suit. However, he did call freely over Three Clubs and I feel that he should either have a six-card suit, in which case he can return to Four Spades, or some value in one of the other suits. So I bid **3NT,** West passes, and now North bids **Four Hearts.** East passes and I have to think again after the sequence:

South	West	North	East
—	—	—	Pass
2♣	Pass	2◇	Double
2♡	3♣	3♠	Pass
3NT	Pass	4♡	Pass
?			

The Alternatives

In view of North's original Two Diamonds, it might be wrong to try for a slam. The most cautious advance would be to Four Spades, as this could be passed by North. More energetic slam tries would be Five Hearts, Five Spades, 4NT, or Five of a minor. Even if we reject a leap to Six Hearts, which would certainly be too bold (though many would do it), the list of alternatives cannot be shortened from:

> Five Spades
> Five Hearts
> Five Diamonds
> Five Clubs
> 4NT
> Four Spades
> Pass

The Choice

Before examining the relative merits of 4NT and calls at the level of Five, we must study whether any slam try is advisable.

Limits of North's Hand

The requirements for a positive response to Two Clubs are not precise in terms of high cards, but I would expect partner to bid Two Spades with A Q 10 x x and a side Queen, and personally I wouldn't wait for the Queen. Having denied even such a modest holding, North will consider himself free, with a mindful partner, to do some bidding thereafter below the game level on quite moderate values. Let's look at a few specimen hands and see how they fit in with the sequence he has adopted:

$$(1) \spadesuit \text{A 9 x x x} \quad \heartsuit \text{Q x x} \quad \diamondsuit \text{x} \quad \clubsuit \text{x x x x}$$

This is the most North could have, and over 3NT a good player would have bid more than Four Hearts. He would bid Five Hearts or perhaps Four Diamonds. With this hand opposite, the slam would normally depend on hearts being 3-2.

$$(2) \spadesuit \text{Q 10 x x x x} \quad \heartsuit \text{J x x} \quad \diamondsuit \text{x x x} \quad \clubsuit \text{x}$$

Another possible holding for partner. He would take out 3NT

because the hand should play for at least one extra trick in hearts. He knows South has a fair heart suit, for otherwise he would not have bid the suit when Two Diamonds was doubled. Here there is not much to choose between Four Hearts and Four Spades, but we would not want to be any higher.

(3) ♠ A x x x x x ♡ J x x ◇ x x ♣ x x

A maximum for partner but still the slam would be no lay-down, with the likelihood of uneven division in the minor suits.

(4) ♠ Q J 10 x x ♡ Q x x x ◇ J x ♣ x x

With heart support of this quality North would have given a clearer picture of his assets by jumping to Four Hearts on the second round.

(5) ♠ A x x x x ♡ J 10 x ◇ x x ♣ J x x

A likely hand, on which again we would be content to stay out of a slam.

The Higher Calls

It is clear from these examples that a slam is unlikely to be comfortable and that it may be dangerous to go beyond the level of Four. The only advance that is at all safe is to Four Spades, which partner will not regard as forcing. Of the higher calls, Five Spades is more dangerous than the rest because it excludes Five Hearts, and 4NT is particularly inept. If intended to be natural, and capable of being passed, it may be too high. If it is a conventional bid, it will solve no problems. I mark the alternatives:

Pass	10
Four Spades	7
Five Hearts	3
Five Diamonds	3
Five Clubs	3
Five Spades	1
4NT	1

Reflections on the Bidding

One of the marks of a good bidder is that he remembers not only partner's last bid, but the one before that, and the one before that as well. This is a good example. It is easy to be distracted by the intervention and the number of bids that have been made, and to forget that partner is thinking all the time, "He knows I bid Two Diamonds to start with."

Another way for South to assess the situation is to reflect that he has a minimum Two Club opening and that not enough has happened to improve his hand. If partner had been able to bid one of the A K x suits, that would have given much better cause for optimism.

3. Study the Type

My partner at rubber bridge is an experienced player but we have no close understanding together. With neither side vulnerable I hold as dealer:

♠ A K 9 6 4   ♡ 8 5 2   ◇ A Q J 4   ♣ 6

I open **One Spade** and he responds **Two Clubs.** I rebid **Two Diamonds** and now he bids **Two Hearts.** This I take to be natural and not the so-called fourth-suit-forcing convention. I have to decide which way to move after the sequence:

South	West	North	East
1♠	Pass	2♣	Pass
2◇	Pass	2♡	Pass
?			

The Alternatives

The change of suit is not forcing, at any rate with my present partner, and I can take the safe part score. Two Spades and 2NT are obvious possibilities and I am going to consider raising the hearts. 3NT would be excessive. If we omit that, the alternatives are:

Three Hearts
2NT
Two Spades
Pass

The Choice

The limits of my partner's hand range from about a shapely 8 points to a maximum of 13 or so. He will not have less than:

(1) ♠ x   ♡ A J x x   ◇ x x   ♣ K 10 x x x x

Nor more than:

(2) ♠ x x   ♡ A K x x   ◇ 10 x   ♣ A Q x x x

It is possible that we cannot make a game anywhere, but there is no reason to assume partner is minimum and I am certainly going to make at least one more call. Partner has responded at the Two level and he was not obliged to bid over Two Diamonds.

Except that it keeps the bidding open, I don't see much merit in Two Spades. One advantage of Two Spades, I admit, is that if partner's next call is 2NT I can show the secondary support for hearts. But, if passed, it will surely be a worse contract than Two Hearts. It will also give partner a wrong picture of my hand. He will place me with something more like:

$$\spadesuit Q J 9 x x x \quad \heartsuit x \quad \diamondsuit A K 10 x x \quad \clubsuit x$$

There must be a better call somewhere.

Why Not 2NT?

We have all the suits covered and may well have the magical 24 points between us, but on the evidence so far there is a misfit and I don't see what suit we are likely to run. Even if partner has a doubleton spade, we shall need a lucky division of the outstanding spades to make anything of them. In addition, my hand is not a no trump type. My partner seems to feel the same about his hand, for otherwise, holding the hearts, he could have bid 2NT on the second round.

What of Three Hearts?

The trump support for what is likely to be a four-card suit is under standard, but I don't imagine he will want to draw trumps. Suppose he has something like:

$$(3) \spadesuit x \quad \heartsuit A Q 9 x \quad \diamondsuit x x \quad \clubsuit K Q x x x x$$

You can sometimes make a lot of tricks with a hand like that, going merrily to and fro. Certainly hearts will play better than no trump.

Since partner can, of course, transfer Three Hearts to 3NT if he wishes, I consider Three Hearts the best call. There is not much to choose between Two Spades and 2NT. I doubt whether it could be right to pass with any partner and I mark the alternatives.

Three Hearts................10
2NT 5
Two Spades................. 3
Pass........................ 2

Reflections on the Bidding

This example is designed to demonstrate two points. The first is that the suitability of a hand for a bid of no trump cannot be judged solely by counting the points. It is necessary to examine the *type* of hand and the fit with partner's suit or suits. Consider the same sequence (One Spade—Two Clubs, Two Diamonds—Two Hearts) when South holds:

♠ K Q J 9 x   ♡ Q x   ◇ A J 10 x   ♣ J x

Fourteen points again, like the original example, but obviously a much better candidate for 2NT. Now there are supporting cards for partner's suits and the spades may develop tricks with very little opposite.

The second point concerns the raise on three small trumps and the willingness to play in game with only seven hearts in the two hands. If this goes against the grain, remember that when you have top cards opposite short suits and expect the play to develop on cross-ruff lines, you can be very happy with support such as A x x or even, as here, x x x.

4. Rare Contribution

In a team event neither side is vulnerable and as dealer I hold:

♠ K J 6 3   ♡ A 3   ◇ K Q 10 2   ♣ 10 9 4

We are playing in theory a weak 1NT of 12 to 14 points. This hand of 13 points qualifies and I open **1NT**. Any other opening would in fact present problems on the rebid. West overcalls with **Two Hearts** and my partner bids **2NT**. East passes and the question is whether I should press on after the sequence:

South	West	North	East
1NT	2♡	2NT	Pass
?			

The Alternatives

I can pass 2NT, raise to game, or make some exploratory bid at the Three level. Some case could be made for Three Spades, Three Hearts or Three Diamonds. I have another suggestion which will appear later, but for the moment we can consider the alternatives to be:

3NT
Three Spades
Three Hearts
Three Diamonds
Pass

The Choice

As weak no trump hands go, this one containing 13 points plus two 10's is by no means a minimum. Had there been no intervention I would not have hesitated to bid the game, for raises to 2NT are always based on the presumption that the opener will bid game unless dead minimum.

After the intervention, I have to allow for various possibilities: that partner has stretched, that he has no heart stop (for that would not necessarily deter him from supporting no trump in this sequence), and that the hand may play better in a suit which he has had to suppress. After my 1NT and the Two Hearts by West he might reasonably bid 2NT on any of the following hands:

(1) ♠ Q 10 x x ♡ 10 x x ◇ A x x ♣ K Q x

(2) ♠ x x ♡ K x ◇ J x x x ♣ A Q J x x

(3) ♠ A x x ♡ Q x ◇ A x x x ♣ J x x x

(4) ♠ x x x ♡ J x ◇ J x x ♣ A K J x x

With a little luck we might make game in spades or no trump on certain of these holdings, but I don't see any method of advance that would enable us consistently to find the right contract. The first conclusion that partner will draw if I introduce a suit at the Three level is that I am nervous about the hearts, probably having no stop. Thus if I take out into Three Spades he will raise to Four not only on hand (1), where we might make it, but also on hand (3), which would play better in no trump.

The Message of Three Hearts

Three Hearts would be an uncommon bid in this sequence and I am not sure what he would make of it. I suppose it would say, "I hold the Ace of hearts but in case you have no guard yourself I am giving you a chance to bid Three Spades." The objection to transmitting that message is that too often, as on hand (4) above, partner would not be able to co-operate in either direction.

Three Diamonds Slightly Safer

If I am to make any call at the Three level, Three Diamonds would give us the best chance of obtaining a plus score. With support for diamonds he could pass and on occasions he would be able to transfer to 3NT.

Prospects of Game Uncertain

Although I have enough in points to bid 3NT I have decided against that because my heart guard is the wrong type. West will open his long heart suit, and I have only the Ace. Besides, partner may have stretched. It is quite likely that he would have passed 1NT. I am not sure that any bid at the Three level would improve our situation and I mark the alternatives:

$$
\begin{array}{ll}
\text{Pass} & 10 \\
\text{Three Diamonds} & 7 \\
\text{Three Hearts} & 6 \\
\text{Three Spades} & 5 \\
\text{3NT} & 5 \\
\end{array}
$$

Reflections on the Bidding

South was in an awkward position here, one that comes up quite often. I seldom make contributions to theory, holding that there are too many conventions already, but it does occur to me that when the responder to 1NT has been prevented by an overcall from employing the Stayman routine (Two Clubs asking for a four-card major) the opener should be able to initiate the conventional enquiry with Three Clubs.

That would be a good way out on the present hand. South bids Three Clubs over 2NT, asking partner to bid a fair suit of spades or diamonds, to bid 3NT if he has a suitable holding in hearts, or to pass if his best suit is clubs. This convention would be especially useful when the opener had no guard in the enemy suit.

5. Unusual Inference

In a pairs event, with both sides vulnerable, I hold as dealer:

♠ 8 2　♡ 4　◇ K Q 5　♣ K J 10 9 7 6 3

At duplicate as well as at rubber bridge I like to make numerous and variable pre-empts and some say that when I catch sight of a seven-card suit I don't look at the rest of the hand. Well, this time I notice the clubs first and I open **Three Clubs.** The club suit is about minimum for a vulnerable Three bid, but there is a trick outside and most players who use weak Three bids in principle would accept this call. After a pass from West my partner responds **Three Hearts.** The opponents remain silent and I have to consider my rebid after the sequence:

South	West	North	East
3♣	Pass	3♡	Pass
?			

The Alternatives

The change of suit after a Three bid is forcing, so a pass is excluded. The weakest call would be Four Clubs. If I want to co-operate in a game try I can bid Four Diamonds or bid the game direct in clubs or no trump. The alternatives are:

> Five Clubs
> Four Clubs
> Four Diamonds
> 3NT

The Choice

Partner's change of suit over the Three bid is unlimited and can cover a wide range of hands. He may be confident of game and thinking of slam in clubs. He may be intending to pass a sign-off of Four Clubs. He may be prepared for 3NT. He may be looking for game in hearts with a suit such as A Q J x x x which wants just a little support.

Too Good to Sign Off

Obviously I cannot raise the hearts, but as I often make Three bids on worse hands than this I prefer not to sign off in Four Clubs. A jump to Five Clubs seems unsuitable when the suit contains two losers and there is a K Q outside.

Four Diamonds Preferable to Five Clubs

Four Diamonds scores over Five Clubs in two respects. It is more informative should partner have his eye on a slam, and it still leaves room for us to play in Four Hearts.

3NT Conveys a Special Inference

The remaining call, 3NT, has the virtue of retaining the option to play in any one of three game contracts. Against it, on the surface, is the fact that the clubs lack two high honors and there is a distinct weakness in spades.

As to the first of these objections, if partner reckon's to make tricks from the clubs he will hold A x or better, so at worst we shall be fishing for the Queen.

The second objection—the weakness in spades—becomes less important if one can assume that partner will draw a neat inference. Had my spades and diamonds been reversed I would have bid Three Spades over Three Hearts, for this is a situation where the pre-emptive opener tries to show partner where his outside strength lies. When I bid 3NT over Three Hearts there is an inference that I am weak in spades. Compare these two possible North hands:

(1) ♠ K 10 x   ♡ A K Q 10 x   ◇ J x   ♣ A x x

(2) ♠ J x   ♡ A K Q 10 x   ◇ J 10 x x   ♣ A Q

On hand (1), since he holds the spades himself, he lets 3NT stand. On hand (2) he takes out 3NT into Four Clubs, which I pass.

If we meet disaster in 3NT because partner has overlooked this particular inference, I can put on a display of One-Upmanship in the post-mortem. This is the bid I select and I mark the alternatives:

26

Reflections on the Bidding

The main interest in this problem lay in the inference that North should draw about South's spade holding.

A similar situation often arises when a player bids 3NT in circumstances that suggest he is taking a chance on one suit. Suppose that South holds:

♠ K x x   ♡ J x   ◇ A Q J x x   ♣ A 9 x

The bidding begins:

South	North
1◇	1♠
2♠	3◇
?	

South will probably bid 3NT now. There is then an inference that his weaker suit is hearts, for had his hearts and clubs been reversed, the bid over Three Diamonds would surely have been Three Hearts.

6. Working Well

My partner at rubber bridge is a capable player. Our side is vulnerable when I deal and pick up:

♠ A Q 10 7 5 4   ♡ Q 8 6 4   ◇ K   ♣ A 5

I open **One Spade** and the opponent on my left overcalls with **Two Hearts.** My partner comes in with **Three Clubs** and East passes. I have to look for a satisfactory rebid after the sequence:

South	West	North	East
1♠	2♡	3♣	Pass
?			

The Alternatives

The main choice is between a simple rebid in spades and a rebid more indicative of my strength. I could jump to Four Spades, I could raise the clubs, and 3NT is a possibility. Three Hearts would be a way to extract some further information from partner. If we include that, the alternatives are:

> Four Spades
> Three Spades
> Four Clubs
> 3NT
> Three Hearts

The Choice

This problem solves itself for players who will say that as partner has come in at the Three level he must have a goodish hand and will surely bid again over Three Spades. That may be good doctrine in some systems, but is not the Acol style. When partner has shown fair values in a competitive situation I must take that into account in choosing my next bid, not sit back and expect him to bid the same cards twice.

In other words, Three Spades on this far from minimum hand

would throw a strain on a partner who had perhaps stretched a little to overcall in the first place.

Four Spades is the obvious alternative, but it might not be the best game contract. My holding in hearts raises a doubt. Unless my partner has a singleton heart, I can foresee West's cashing his top hearts and then giving his partner a ruff. After that there might be another loser for us in spades or diamonds.

Four Clubs is open to the same objection, that it might play unluckily after a heart lead. In any case Five Clubs will be better than Four Spades only when partner is very short of spades.

All Cards Working in No Trump

In 3NT the four hearts to the Queen will cease to be a liability. Tricks may come from either suit, spades or clubs. Playing in spades, I might be cut off from dummy's clubs and unable to dispose of my heart losers.

The singleton King of diamonds does not strike me as a serious drawback. West will hardly lead the Ace of diamonds even if he has it. Actually, the King of diamonds is likely to be a much more useful card in no trump than in spades, whether partner holds the Ace or not.

Would Three Hearts Solve Any Problems?

Yes, to the extent that it would enable us to choose more accurately between spades and clubs. Played according to the modern style, Three Hearts would not confirm clubs but would promise game values and request partner to declare himself further. With K x or J x x in spades he would show that support, with K x in hearts he would bid 3NT, and if unable to do either of those he would probably repeat his clubs.

Compare these two hands:

(1) ♠ x x   ♡ x x   ◇ A x x   ♣ K Q 10 x x x

(2) ♠ x   ♡ x x   ◇ A x x x   ♣ K Q 10 9 x x

On hand (1) he would respond Four Clubs to Three Hearts and would pass my next bid of Four Spades. On hand (2) he would go to Five Clubs over Four Spades, having drawn the inference that my spades were not solid.

29

Three Hearts is an improvement on Four Spades, therefore, but too often it would lead to our by-passing 3NT, which, it will be observed, would be the best spot on either of the hands above. Judging 3NT to be the contract in which my hand will be most effective, I mark the alternatives:

$$
\begin{array}{lr}
\text{3NT} & 10 \\
\text{Three Hearts} & 7 \\
\text{Four Spades} & 5 \\
\text{Three Spades} & 4 \\
\text{Four Clubs} & 3 \\
\end{array}
$$

Reflections on the Bidding

Questions of partnership understanding entered into this problem, but whatever one's interpretation of Three Spades or Three Hearts, the analysis ending in preference for 3NT is, I think, instructive. Apart from the spade suit itself, all the features of South's hand are designed for 3NT rather than Four Spades.

Many players would fail to consider 3NT because of the singleton King. There they miscalculate. For the most part—and especially when the main strength is on the declarer's left—a singleton King will play the same role as K x.

What Would Seven Clubs Mean?

It would give partner a chance to show the King of diamonds if he had it, but in general he would read the bid as a request to choose between Seven Hearts and 7NT, not between hearts and spades. Since he wouldn't bid 7NT without one of the minor suit Kings, Seven Clubs must be given a slight edge over Seven Hearts and I mark the alternatives:

> Seven Clubs..................10
> Seven Hearts 9
> 7NT 4
> Seven Spades................ 3

Reflections on the Bidding

This problem has quite a history. Back in 1952 the two hands were presented in *The New York Times* as follows:

South	*North*
♠ K Q 6 3	♠ A J 10 9 5
♡ A J 9 5 2	♡ K Q 10 6
◇ A 10	◇ Q 6 3
♣ A J	♣ 4

The writer of the column, Albert Morehead, remarked that as the bidding had gone it was very difficult for South to visualize that the grand slam should be bid in hearts, not spades. A long article in the *Bridge World* argued that it was not so difficult, and Morehead, admitting this, six years later put the hand to the *Bridge World* panel of experts. The combined votes for Seven Spades and 7NT again outnumbered Seven Hearts, and the merit of Seven Clubs was not acknowledged, though there were a few votes for that call.

When there is a choice between two trump suits of equal length, either both 5-4 or both 5-3, the question to ask is: *Which hand will benefit from a discard?* In the present example, South, with his two doubletons, was sure to benefit from a discard on the fifth spade.

8. Providing the Tricks

At rubber bridge I deal and pick up:

♠ J   ♡ A K 7 4   ◇ A 8 4   ♣ A Q 7 4 2

Neither side is vulnerable and I open **One Club.** Partner responds **One Spade** and I reverse with **Two Hearts.** Partner repeats his suit, **Two Spades.** The question is how close we are to game after the sequence:

South	West	North	East
1♣	Pass	1♠	Pass
2♡	Pass	2♠	Pass
?			

The Alternatives

Partner's rebid is limited, and I could pass Two Spades. The obvious bids in the medium range are 2NT and Three Spades. I could try the effect of Three Diamonds or I could bid game from hand with 3NT or Four Spades. If the problem were put to several players their answers would cover this wide range:

> Four Spades
> Three Spades
> 3NT
> 2NT
> Three Diamonds
> Pass

The Choice

My reverse of Two Hearts promised a better than minimum hand, but was not forcing after a response at the range of One. Partner has made about the weakest bid available. He could be no better than:

(1) ♠ A 10 8 x x x   ♡ x x   ◇ J x x   ♣ x x

Now Two Spades would be quite high enough. That is sufficient to show that a jump to Four Spades or, still worse, 3NT would be unsound, but it does not follow that game hopes should be abandoned.

North could have a more useful hand, such as:

(2) ♠ K Q 10 x x x ♡ Q x ◇ x x x ♣ x x

Or:

(3) ♠ K 10 9 x x x ♡ x x x ◇ J x ♣ K x

Four Spades would be a good contract with either of these hands. [Some players would say that hand (1) was worth a jump to Three Spades over the reverse, but in my opinion that would be exaggerated.]

There would similarly be a good play for 3NT if North held:

(4) ♠ A Q 10 x x ♡ x x x ◇ Q x x ♣ 10 x

Because of the diamond position it would be better for North to be the declarer at no trump. That is one argument for Three Diamonds or Three Spades on my hand in preference to 2NT. There are others. A bid of 2NT will give partner the impression that I am relying on my own hand for tricks at no trump, rather than on his spades. On many hands he will bid 3NT when we would be better off in Four Spades.

What Would Three Diamonds Mean?

If one had a close understanding with partner concerning a bid of the fourth suit it might be possible to bid Three Diamonds as a request to him to make one more descriptive bid—either 3NT or a repeat of the spades or delayed support for one of the other suits. However, in rubber bridge the sequence would be a little ambiguous; partner might take it as a genuine suit and bid on the assumption that South was void of spades. Also, if North bid Three Spades over Three Diamonds, South would not know whether to bid the fourth.

Because of this uncertainty I judge Three Spades to be the best call. Some credit must be given to a pass, because sometimes eight tricks will be the limit. Any jump to game would be an overbid and also might land the partnership in the wrong game. I mark the alternatives:

Three Spades	10
Three Diamonds	6
2NT	6
Pass	5
Four Spades	3
3NT	1

Reflections on the Bidding

Experience has shown many times that when the player with the strong hand has a singleton of partner's long suit he should aim to play in the trump contract and not at no trump.

It is true that when two poor bidders meet this kind of situation they surmount it successfully. The big hand bids no trump and the weak hand invariably takes out into the long suit!

A standard example occurs when the bidding between two such partners begins Three Spades—3NT and always the first player goes back to Four Spades. Sometimes 3NT will be the right contract and players who bid in this style can never stop there.

When the bidding between two good players goes:

South	*North*
1♣	1♠
2♡	2♠
3NT	

South's 3NT says one of two things, either:

"I have enough strength in spades to bring in your suit."

Or:

"I have a strong suit of my own and expect to make nine tricks without the use of your spades. Don't take me back!"

9. Playing the Field

In a team-of-four match my partner is a good player but we are not an experienced combination and have no very close understanding. Neither side is vulnerable. First to speak I hold:

♠ A Q 6 4   ♡ 7   ◇ J 10 6 3 2   ♣ 7 5 4

I pass, the next player passes, and my partner opens **One Club.** After a pass by East I respond **One Diamond.** Partner rebids 2NT, which in our system suggests about 16 to 18 points in high cards. East passes and the question is whether I should try for game after the sequence:

South	West	North	East
Pass	Pass	1♣	Pass
1◇	Pass	2NT	Pass
?			

The Alternatives

In terms of points we seem to be on the borderline between 2NT and 3NT. Because of the distribution, it may be advisable to explore ways of playing in a suit contract, possibly below the game level. Three Spades, a new suit, would be forcing. Three Diamonds, in our system, would be discouraging. The forcing quality of Three Clubs, after the original pass, is less certain. These seem to be the alternatives:

3NT
Three Spades
Three Diamonds
Three Clubs
Pass

The Choice

Crediting my partner with an average 17 points for his rebid of 2NT, and adding that to my 7, I estimate that in terms of points we should be in the game zone at no trump. However, my hand has structural defects that make 3NT highly dubious. Change the position of the spade and diamond honors and I would bid 3NT without hesitation on:

$$\spadesuit \; J \; 10 \; 6 \; 4 \quad \heartsuit \; 7 \quad \diamondsuit \; A \; Q \; 6 \; 3 \; 2 \quad \clubsuit \; 7 \; 5 \; 4$$

As things are, partner may need two honors in diamonds and a double stop in hearts to make 3NT. I am not going to attempt 3NT without further exploration, therefore. Nor do I like passing the bid of 2NT. For one thing, there may be a sound game somewhere. For another, that contract may fail if there is a long heart suit against us. No doubt partner has a stop, but he may still have to lose five hearts and perhaps another trick while establishing my diamonds. It should be possible to find a better call among the suits that can be bid at the level of Three.

Three Diamonds

In Acol this rebid is a sign-off, or at least a warning that the responder has doubts about 3NT and is prepared to stop short of game. That makes it a poor bid here, for partner will be more inclined to pass if he has a doubleton in diamonds, and there is no reason to think that Three Diamonds will be an improvement on 2NT.

Three Spades

This has certain merits. In the first place, partner can hold four spades even though he didn't bid them. He is not one of those scientific players who never by-pass a four-card major. Second, I have made ten tricks before now with a trump holding of A Q x x opposite K x x.

An additional point is that if he cannot support spades, partner does not have to bid 3NT, although he can if he is well upholstered in hearts. Instead he can transfer to Four Diamonds or Four Clubs, either of which should be playable.

The disadvantage of Three Spades is that it takes us beyond the range of Three Clubs or Three Diamonds. That is why we must look closely at the next bid.

Three Clubs

This return to partner's suit over 2NT is classified in our system as forcing for one round. Whether it is forcing after my original pass is a matter I have not discussed with my partner, but I think he would feel free to pass Three Clubs on a hand not too promising for 3NT, such as:

(1) ♠ K 10 x ♡ A x x x ◇ K x ♣ A Q J x

Or:

(2) ♠ K x x ♡ Q 10 x ◇ A x ♣ A K J x x

If he does not intend to pass Three Clubs, several bids are available. Three Diamonds, Three Hearts and 3NT are obvious possibilities and, on a certain type of hand, Four Clubs might come into the reckoning.

Whether forcing or not, Three Clubs leaves partner with a wide range of calls and should at any rate lead to a plus score. Three Spades must be better than 3NT, and I mark the alternatives:

Three Clubs 10
Three Spades................. 7
3NT 5
Pass....................... 4
Three Diamonds............. 2

Reflections on the Bidding

In some systems—standard American, for example—the rebid of 2NT would show greater strength than it does in Acol and South's problem would be different. The point of the discussion nevertheless remains valid. When the choice seems to be close between various bids, the one that leaves open the way to the greatest number of likely contracts is apt to be the best. Thus, in the present example, Three Clubs does not exclude a final contract of Three Clubs (if that can be passed) or Three Diamonds or 3NT or Four of a minor. Three Spades leaves open the way to 3NT or Four Spades or Four of a minor. The other calls operate within a much more restricted field.

10. A New Look

In a pairs event I note that a rather stolid-looking couple have come to our table. While I am thinking about this and that, I see that, with no one vulnerable, I have to speak first on:

♠ K J   ♡ A 5   ◇ K 9 8 6 2   ♣ 10 7 4 3

Disdaining the customary gambit to the effect that I didn't realize it was my deal, I open, guiltily, **One Diamond.** West overcalls with **One Heart,** my partner bids **One Spade,** and a raise to **Two Hearts** by East happily relieves me of the necessity to find a rebid. However, I am not off the hook for long. After two passes my partner reopens with a jump to **Four Diamonds,** and I have to take another look at my hand after this sequence:

South	West	North	East
1◇	1♡	1♠	2♡
Pass	Pass	4◇	Pass
?			

The Alternatives

Partner's jump is not altogether forcing so having opened light I am free to pass. Since my few high cards may be well placed, I can play for game in either Four Spades or Five Diamonds. By bidding Four Hearts I might perhaps induce partner to choose between those two contracts. The alternatives are:

Five Diamonds
Four Spades
Four Hearts
Pass

The Choice

At most tables, it is charitable to assume, South will have passed originally. My opening bid may have turned out luckily. If Four Diamonds, scoring 130 or 150, is going to be a good result, I don't need to improve on it.

West probably hasn't got an opening bid, but North, holding a spade suit and enough for a double jump in diamonds, probably does. Had West and I passed, he surely would have opened with One Spade. What would have happened then? I would have responded Two Diamonds, he would presumably have raised to Three, and I would have tried Three Spades. Thus I cannot take the comfortable view that we already have a good score owing to my irregular opening.

The Hand Has Improved

I might pass for a different reason—that I had opened sub-minimum and had no excuse for bidding again unless forced to. That is a shallow sort of argument. Revaluing my hand as the bidding progresses, I conclude that all my 11 points are fully operational. The 13 or 14 points of many a sound opening dwindle to 6 or 7 working points after a round or two of bidding, but my assets, such as they are, have increased in w⌐rth!

Game in Spades or Diamonds?

This I find difficult to judge. Partner is more likely to have five spades than six, for with six he might have preferred Three Spades on the second round. He must have high cards as well as distribution, for otherwise the opponents would not have subsided at Two Hearts. Let's look at some possible hands he might hold:

(1) ♠ A Q x x x ♡ x x ♢ A J x x ♣ J x

Not much to choose between the game at spades or diamonds. We cannot afford to lose a diamond in either contract.

(2) ♠ A x x x x ♡ x x x ♢ Q J x x ♣ A

This might be grisly in Four Spades, but Five Diamonds would be fairly safe. Perhaps he wouldn't let Four Spades stand.

(3) ♠ A Q x x ♡ x x ♢ Q J 9 x ♣ A 10 x

Now he would certainly transfer Four Spades to Five Diamonds, remembering that I did not raise to Two Spades on the previous round.

Four Spades will also be the more popular contract because of the match-point factor, and if only for that reason I ought not to go beyond it.

41

Is Four Hearts a Solution?

Four Hearts would be cute if partner could be relied on to take it as a request to choose between Four Spades and Five Diamonds. The objection is that he might read it as a slam try, my hand having been greatly improved by the raise in diamonds. I am not so much concerned about his carrying me to Six Diamonds (which might even make!) as about his by-passing Four Spades. It might not occur to him to repeat anything less than a six-card suit.

I conclude with regret that Four Hearts would not be entirely sound, and I mark the alternatives:

> Four Spades.................10
> Five Diamonds 7
> Four Hearts................. 7
> Pass........................ 4

Reflections on the Bidding

The choice between the three bids at the finish was close and the main interest of the hand lies in South's decision not to pass. This was reached in two stages. First, he had to work out that although his unsound opening seemed to have turned out well, other pairs might be in game. Second, he had to forget that his opening bid was sub-minimum and revalue his hand in the light of later developments.

11. Encouraging Sign

In a team event I am third to speak and hold:

♠ 5 ♡ J 9 8 6 3 2 ◇ K 8 ♣ A Q 10 4

Neither side is vulnerable and my partner opens **One Diamond.**
East, on my right, overcalls with **One Spade** and I come in with **Two
Hearts.** West raises his partner to **Two Spades,** my partner bids
Three Diamonds, and East passes. The question is which way to
move after the sequence:

South	West	North	East
—	—	1◇	1♠
2♡	2♠	3◇	Pass
?			

The Alternatives

Any game bid would be excessive, but I could test partner's reaction
to Four Diamonds or Four Clubs. If I judge game in diamonds to be
remote, I can repeat my hearts or pass. The remaining possibility is
Three Spades—an attempt to manoeuvre partner into 3NT if he can
control the spades. That makes five calls to be considered:

Four Diamonds
Four Clubs
Three Spades
Three Hearts
Pass

The Choice

The intervention by both opponents has deprived us of bidding
space and I cannot tell whether partner would have made a jump rebid
had we been left to ourselves. Probably not, but he must be better

43

than minimum to rebid freely at the Three level. He won't have less than:

$$(1) \spadesuit \, J \, x \quad \heartsuit \, Q \, x \quad \diamondsuit \, A \, Q \, J \, 9 \, x \, x \quad \clubsuit \, K \, x \, x$$

The fact that he has not supported my hearts is, in its way, an encouraging sign. If he has a singleton heart the fit in diamonds will be that much better. There would be a good chance for Five Diamonds if he held no more than:

$$(2) \spadesuit \, x \, x \, x \quad \heartsuit \, K \quad \diamondsuit \, A \, Q \, 10 \, 9 \, x \, x \quad \clubsuit \, K \, J \, x$$

The prospects for game are surely good enough to justify a further call.

Three Hearts

The bid that appeals least is Three Hearts. Partner cannot go on bidding his own hand forever and if he has a singleton heart he may have to pass. That is one of the few ways in which we could end up with a minus score. Failure to rebid hearts now does not, of course, exclude the possibility of our reaching Four Hearts.

Four Diamonds

One of the merits of this bid is that it gives partner a good opportunity to show secondary support for hearts. Four Diamonds also seems about right on values and the information about the King of diamonds may be what North most needs to know. So far, I see no objection to this call.

Four Clubs

The information that I have values in clubs would probably be more useful to my partner if he knew about my King of diamonds. Otherwise, I feel that we shall be battling in the dark. If over Four Clubs he bids Four Hearts or Five Clubs, I shall be uncertain whether or not to transfer to Five Diamonds; and if he bids Four Diamonds, I shall have no idea whether or not to raise. In that sense Four Clubs is a trap bid.

Three Spades

The main purpose of this call would be to extract 3NT from partner if he held this sort of hand:

(3) ♠ Q J x ♡ 10 x ♢ A Q J 10 x x ♣ K x

Now 3NT is the only game we can make. However, I feel that this is a long shot and the bid is open to the same objection as Four Clubs—that if it produces a bid of Four Diamonds from North, I shall be no further on.

Summing Up

To bid Three Spades or Four Clubs now and follow with Five Diamonds would make my hand sound stronger than it is. (For example, if Four Clubs were raised to Five and I then bid Five Diamonds, partner would conclude that I was angling for Six.) It occurs to me that a direct raise to Five Diamonds would be as good as some of the calls we have been looking at. Putting the interloper in brackets, I mark the alternatives:

Four Diamonds 10
Three Spades 6
Four Clubs 5
(Five Diamonds . . . . 5)
Three Hearts 3
Pass 3

Reflections on the Bidding

This was a fairly straightforward exercise in constructive bidding, but two general points emerge.

First, there was the expectation of a good fit in diamonds arising from partner's temporary denial of hearts. When it looks as though partner may have a singleton of your Jack-high suit, that is an indication that his high cards in other suits will fit well with yours. By contrast, a holding such as K Q x x x in a suit where partner may be short is a bad sign.

Second, the objection raised against the bids of Three Spades and Four Clubs is, I think, instructive. South knows that the partnership is close to Five Diamonds, and the way to obtain co-operation from partner is to tell him so by raising the diamonds—not to make an uninformative call that may force him to bid Four Diamonds and still leave you none the wiser

The same principle often arises for the defending side. With both sides vulnerable, an opponent opens One Club and you overcall One Spade, holding:

$$\spadesuit A Q 8 6 4 \quad \heartsuit J 6 \quad \diamondsuit A 10 9 6 3 \quad \clubsuit 4$$

Partner bids Two Hearts. Now if there is game at all it is likely to be in Four Hearts and you should raise to Three. It is a mistake to bid Three Diamonds and then not know what to do when partner repeats his hearts.

12. A Slam Philosophy

Playing in a team event, with neither side vulnerable, I hold as dealer:

♠ A Q J ♡ K 9 2 ◇ A J 6 3 2 ♣ J 6

I open **One Diamond** and partner responds **One Heart.** That gives me a slightly awkward rebid. A simple raise to Two Hearts would suggest, in our system, not much better than a minimum opening, and here I have 16 points in high cards plus a ruffing value and a five-card suit. The hand is actually midway between Two Hearts and Three Hearts. The best measure for the moment may be to temporize with **One Spade.** This elicits **3NT** from partner, which I take to show about 13 to 15 points. The question is whether I should try for a slam after the sequence:

South	West	North	East
1◇	Pass	1♡	Pass
1♠	Pass	3NT	Pass
?			

The Alternatives

I could let the bidding rest at 3NT. Four Hearts is a possibility and so is 4NT (natural, not conventional). I could bid Four Diamonds to see what that would produce. A more direct slam suggestion would be Five Hearts. I wouldn't consider anything higher than that, so the alternatives are:

Five Hearts
Four Hearts
4NT (natural)
Four Diamonds
Pass

The Choice

Partner's minimum is a hand just too good for a non-forcing 2NT and his maximum is a hand just short of a force. This could be 15 or a moderate 16 (counting high cards alone). It is clear that if he is not much better than minimum there will be no play for a slam, and a game contract such as 3NT or Four Hearts will be enough. If he is maximum and fits well, there could be a slam. Six Hearts would be a fair venture if he had either of these hands:

(1) ♠ 10 x x ♡ A Q x x x ◇ K x ♣ A Q x

(2) ♠ x x ♡ A 10 x x x x ◇ K ♣ A Q 10 x

What I have to decide is whether there is a safe way of approaching any slam there may be. I don't want to languish at the Five level, or even the Four level, and then go down!

Without stopping to construct possible hands that my partner may hold, I know that 4NT, with a combined 29 or 30 points, would be no certainty against a bad break. In addition, the heart support in my hand is likely to be an important element in any slam, so that any try that concealed that support would be unsatisfactory.

Would Four Hearts Be a Slam Try?

That's a point I haven't discussed directly with my present partner, but it seems uncertain. Take a hand of this type:

♠ A Q x x ♡ J x x ◇ A Q x x x ♣ x

After the same bidding sequence of One Diamond—One Heart—One Spade—3NT, Four Hearts would be the natural bid on this far weaker hand.

A second question is whether Four Hearts would always be safe. It could fail if there were two losers in the trump suit.

Would Four Diamonds Lead Anywhere?

Unlikely. If partner bid Four Hearts or Five Diamonds I still wouldn't be confident about going any higher.

The answer to the hand seems to be that it is difficult to find a slam try that will not be too forceful and will at the same time convey the heart support. Since Four Hearts would not be a clear slam try and might not be so safe a contract as 3NT, I mark the alternatives:

```
Pass........................10
Four Hearts................. 8
4NT ....................... 4
Four Diamonds.............. 4
Five Hearts ................ 2
```

Reflections on the Bidding

Different systems would tackle this hand in a different and perhaps more satisfactory way. It happens to be an awkward hand for my system, the way the bidding has gone, and the value of the example lies in the mental approach toward the possibility of making a slam try.

Analysis of match records almost always shows more points lost than won by attempts to reach borderline slams. That is because players move too quickly to the question, "What slam try shall I make?" They forget to ask themselves first whether any slam try is safe and whether, if they reach a slam, they can be reasonably sure of playing in the right suit.

No partnership is good enough to bid all the slams that come its way. The sensible policy is to bid the obvious ones and let the rest escape.

PART TWO

Doubles—Competitive, Co-operative and Crass!

In the following group of hands the question of whether to double (or accept partner's double) comes strongly into consideration. It is a department of the game where even top-notch players sometimes fail badly in their judgment. In the examples dealing with close doubles I draw attention to questions that are often overlooked, such as:

Does my hand contain any unpleasant surprise for the declarer?

Can I form a clear picture of how the defence is likely to go?

If the double is in any sense co-operative, has my partner sufficient information on which to decide intelligently whether to let the double stand?

Must I risk the double (in a match-pointed event) in order to have a chance of a good score?

13. Never Return

With both sides vulnerable in a keenly fought rubber, I deal and hold this awkward hand:

♠ — ♡ Q J 8 7 ◇ J 8 6 5 2 ♣ A K Q 4

There are three possible opening bids, and it might even be a good idea to pass and judge later what action to take.

The call I find easiest to reject is One Heart. The hand is not strong enough to be bid as a three-suiter and I am prepared to let the hearts go unless partner can mention them.

As between One Diamond and One Club, there could be advantage in calling the suit where the top cards are, but sometimes it works the other way. Moreover, a sequence such as One Club—One Spade would be difficult to handle.

After thinking so long I can't very well pass, so **One Diamond** it is. The opponent on my left bids **Three Spades,** my partner **doubles,** and the next hand passes. Does that suit me or not, the bidding having gone:

South	West	North	East
1◇	3♠	Double	Pass
?			

The Alternatives

If I take the double out, the obvious bid is Four Clubs, but 3NT is also a possibility. Four Hearts would sound too strong, so the alternatives are:

Four Clubs
3NT
Pass

The Choice

The void in spades is no reason for taking out a double at this level. I am worried more by the indifferent quality of my diamond suit.

51

An opening lead of the King of diamonds from K x would certainly be an unhappy start to the defence.

On the surface, I should be regretting that I opened One Diamond and not One Club, but there is another way of looking at it. If I had opened One Club, partner might have counted on tricks from a diamond holding of his own such as A K 10 x. It is always a shock to open a short suit that has not been bid and see the first lead ruffed!

My hand contains defensive values in hearts and clubs and for all I know partner may have several tricks in spades. The suit could be divided 8-4-1-0, or something of that sort. I have no reason to despair of our chances of beating Three Spades, but before I decide to leave the double in, I must consider whether there is a satisfactory take-out.

The Rescue Bids

I don't suppose we would go far wrong in Four Clubs. If partner is short of diamonds he should have at least three clubs and possibly more. The suit could break badly against us, though.

3NT would be a wild venture. Where would the tricks come from? It is not as though I had a long and solid suit anywhere.

Who Can Tell?

Defending against Three Spades doubled may be our best spot. The fact is that from my side of the table I cannot tell. Partner, on the other hand, may be entirely confident, and for that reason I think it is sensible to accept his decision. If I rescue into a losing contract when we could have set them 800, he won't be interested in my explanations. I am going to pass and I mark the alternatives:

Pass 10
Four Clubs 6
3NT 2

Reflections on the Bidding

When you are doubtful about leaving in a double, lack of a high honor in the suit you have bid is a disadvantage, certainly, but one that players tend to exaggerate. Often partner has a low singleton, and the lead does no active harm. What *is* dangerous is possession of a long unbid suit headed by the Jack or 10. Partner often has A K x x or A K Q alone of this suit, and the expected tricks tend to disappear.

As to the psychological aspect, I cannot express this better than the Dutch player, Herman Filarski, when the problem was put to him:

"Pass. Because I remember West hands with seven or eight spades and North with A K 10 8 x. Take out such a double and you never can go back in that club again. Three Spades doubled and made is a smaller risk and, moreover, you can say: 'Partner, you should not have doubled.'"

14. They Lose Weight

Playing in a team-of-four match I hold in third position:

♠ J 8   ♡ K Q 10 7   ◇ 9 6   ♣ K J 10 5 3

We are vulnerable and my partner opens **One Spade.** East overcalls with **Two Hearts,** which I am happy to **double.** West takes out into **Three Diamonds,** North passes and so does East. The question is what further move I can make, the bidding having gone:

South	West	North	East
—	—	1♠	2♡
Double	3◇	Pass	Pass
?			

The Alternatives

I can pass or double. If I bid on, it will have to be Three Spades or Four Clubs, or perhaps Three Hearts, with the idea of extracting a further bid from partner. If we include that, the alternatives become:

Four Clubs
Three Spades
Three Hearts
Double
Pass

The Choice

Let's begin by disposing of the idea that Three Hearts is a practical possibility. Following a penalty double of Two Hearts, it could be taken as a genuine suit, such as A Q 10 x x x. I can't risk that, vulnerable.

Now what conclusions can we draw about North's hand? Probably two or three small hearts, for East is likely to have six and West a void or singleton.

North won't have much in diamonds, either in length or strength. If he had either, he would have doubled Three Diamonds.

As he is short in both red suits, it is safe to assume that he has five spades and he may well have six. He would not rush in with Three Spades because I might be short and might be waiting to double Three Diamonds. As to clubs, he will have at least two, and possibly three or four. These are some possible holdings:

(1) ♠ A Q x x x x　♡ x x　♢ K x　♣ Q x x

(2) ♠ A K 10 x x　♡ J x　♢ A x　♣ x x x x

(3) ♠ K Q 9 x x x　♡ x x x　♢ J x　♣ A Q

One point that is immediately obvious is that opponents might well make Three Diamonds. It would be quite unsound to double.

What about Four Clubs? Probably one down, possibly more. The obvious danger is that opponents will begin with Ace of hearts and a heart ruff and then cash two diamonds unless North has the Ace. If North has the King, as in hand (1), it may well be under the Ace.

With the hands shown above, Three Spades will also go down more often than not. Of course, North could be stronger. Suppose that he held:

(4) ♠ A K 10 x x x　♡ x x　♢ x x　♣ A Q x

Now there would be a fair chance of Three Spades, and Three Diamonds would be a make for the other side. The trouble here is that North, expecting more, would bid Four Spades and go down.

Time to Go Quietly

We are left with a pass, which may seem timid opposite an opening bid, but at the vulnerability is probably the right course. Maybe they will make 130 when we could have lost 100 in Three Spades, but that is not serious. We don't want to lose 200—still less to double them out in Three Diamonds. This is how I mark the alternatives:

Pass	10
Three Spades	6
Four Clubs	4
Double	1
Three Hearts	0

55

Reflections on the Bidding

This is a situation where a player's better judgment might tell him that he had no sound bid except a pass, but not many players would respond to their better judgment.

There is a type of semi-expert who would add up his ten points, plus two 10's, decide that opponents could not make nine tricks, and double. As we have seen, that is likely to be disastrous. It should be evident that the heart honors are not going to pull any weight in defence.

The objection to Three Spades is more subtle. We might have enough to make Three Spades, but when that is the case partner will almost surely bid Four. If, as partners do, he says in the post-mortem, "Why didn't you bid Three Spades? We could have made that," the answer is that you could not have stopped there.

15. Neutral Meaning

Playing in a match-pointed pairs tournament against opponents who are good judges, I hold as dealer:

♠ K 8 6 4 2   ♡ A K 6 3   ◇ 7 2   ♣ Q 8

Both sides are vulnerable, and if there were an interval between my suits—if I had spades and diamonds instead of spades and hearts—I wouldn't open, with the prospect of perhaps having to rebid such indifferent spades. As it is, that situation will not arise. Holding spades and hearts, I can rebid in hearts if partner responds at the Two level. So I open **One Spade**. West, on my left, overcalls with **Two Diamonds**. Partner bids **Four Spades** and East contests with **Five Diamonds**. I have to make what is likely to be a critical decision after this sequence:

South	West	North	East
1♠	2◇	4♠	5◇
?			

The Alternatives

Clearly I might pass or double or bid Five Spades. A case can also be made for Five Hearts, so the possibilities are:

Five Spades
Five Hearts
Double
Pass

The Choice

I must say a word first about partner's raise to Four Spades. We are playing the Swiss convention in which One Spade—pass—Four Clubs shows the values for a raise to game, with more in high cards than when the bidding goes One Spade—pass—Four Spades. When there has been an overcall at the Two level, that convention does not apply because Four Clubs may be needed in a natural sense. Also, one may not want to make it plain to the defenders whether the raise is on values or partly pre-emptive.

Thus, partner's hand can be of more than one type. He may have three tricks in high cards, or he may have no more than one. East's hand is also something of an unknown quantity. He may be full value for his raise or he may have taken a chance on a hand worth not more than about Three Diamonds.

Thus the relative strength of the two sides is somewhat obscure. I must bid according to probability, and here, surely, the plain probability is that we have a better chance of making three tricks in defence than eleven in attack. I would bid on at this point if I thought that:

We had a good chance of making 11 tricks.

Or:

They were likely to make their contract.

Or:

The decision was so close that it would be right to bid one trick more "for safety."

This last consideration applies less to match-pointed events than to total points. At rubber bridge the risk of a double swing—allowing opponents to make a game when you could have made game yourself—must be avoided at all costs. In a pairs event it will already be bad if you go down one when you could have defeated the opponents. You must play for the best result, not for safety.

As I don't think that we have any prospect of making eleven tricks unless partner can bid again, and as I have no special reason to suppose that they can make their contract, I am certainly not going to bid Five Spades or Five Hearts in front of my partner. (The main point of Five Hearts, as against Five Spades, is that this would indicate the best lead to partner should we eventually defend against Six Diamonds doubled.) The decision, therefore, lies between a double and a pass.

What Message Would a Double Convey?

The answer to this question is not so self-evident as it may seem. Many players, when their side has opened the bidding and presumably has the balance of the cards, double expressly as a warning to their partners not to bid on. I prefer to attach a more neutral meaning, so that the double in this sequence would say: "So far as I can judge at the moment, we are more likely to defeat Five Diamonds than to make Five Spades."

As that expresses my feeling about this hand, I am satisfied with a double here. I am not by any means counselling my partner against bidding Five Spades if he thinks we can make it, or even if he is so lacking in defence as to be nervous about Five Diamonds. He should go to Five Spades from strength if he holds:

(1) ♠ A Q J x   ♡ Q 10 x x   ◇ x   ♣ A x x x

Lacking defensive tricks, he can take out if he is so unbalanced as:

(2) ♠ A Q 10 x x   ♡ x x x   ◇ —   ♣ J 10 x x x

Even now we might beat Five Diamonds with a spade and two hearts, but we might also make Five Spades.

The case against passing over Five Diamonds is that on many border-line hands partner would go to Five Spades when there would be a better chance of a plus score defending against Five Diamonds. Nevertheless, it is better to pass than to bid Five Spades, and I mark the alternatives:

Double	10
Pass.........................	5
Five Spades	2
Five Hearts	2

Reflections on the Bidding

This was a clear decision because of the disposition of South's honor cards. Had he held A K of spades and King of hearts the situation would have been more open and it would have been right to pass and leave the decision entirely to partner. The Queen of clubs, in particular, was a card more likely to tell in defence than in attack. The only time opponents will make Five Diamonds is when North has long hearts and your apparent tricks in that suit do not materialize.

The main point of this problem is that a double in this sequence does not say, "Don't bid on!" It simply says, "On the information I have so far, I think we should defend rather than bid any higher."

While I do not recommend Five Hearts here, it is worth noting that if South expected to make eleven tricks it would be a sound tactical manoeuvre to show partner where his top tricks lay.

16. The Net

In a team-of-four match my opponents are vulnerable and East, on my right, deals and opens **One Spade**. My hand is:

♠ A Q 10 6 2   ♡ K 7 6   ◇ 8 6 5   ♣ 6 4

I pass, awaiting better things. West passes and my partner **doubles**. Better things on the way! East passes and so do I. West attempts a rescue action with **1NT**. Partner passes and East transfers to **Two Diamonds**. I have to decide whether they have escaped our net after the sequence:

South	West	North	East
—	—	—	1♠
Pass	Pass	Double	Pass
Pass	1NT	Pass	2◇
?			

The Alternatives

If prepared to defend against Two Diamonds, I can double or pass the bid up to my partner. I can compete with Two Spades, the suit bid on my right, or possibly with Two Hearts, as partner is likely to have some length in the suit. The alternatives are:

Two Spades
Two Hearts
Double
Pass

The Choice

The bidding has been fairly informative. My partner has doubled in the protective position but he cannot be particularly strong or he would have doubled West's 1NT after my penalty pass. West is obviously weak, with a singleton or void in spades. East could have five spades and five diamonds but as he passed over the double he is more likely to be 5-4 or 6-4. Also, there is hardly room for him to hold five diamonds. My partner, for his take-out double, is likely to hold three diamonds.

West, who taken out One Spade doubled into 1NT, will surely hold three or four diamonds, and I have three. So, the odds are that the suit is 4-3-3-3 round the table.

How Will the Hand Play in Diamonds?

For East, badly. If he tries to ruff spades in dummy he will be soon overruffed by my partner (the fact that I have no diamond honors is a good sign). If he draws trumps he will have several spades to dispose of. Our side must hold enough cards in clubs and hearts to prevent declarer from making many tricks in those suits.

Against Two Diamonds doubled I plan to lead a club rather than a trump, for I anticipate that partner's trumps will be useful for overruffing the dummy in spades. Partner will return clubs and declarer will soon have to ruff in front of my 8 6 5 of diamonds.

Partner is not bound to leave the double in if he is weaker in defence than his bidding so far has suggested. For example, if he has only a doubleton diamond he can take out into Two Hearts or even Two Spades—remembering that I was anxious to defend against One Spade.

The Other Calls

As between Two Spades and Two Hearts, I would be on safer ground with Two Spades. If I had to guess, I would say that we would average to make eight tricks in spades. We might do better or worse in hearts, depending on the division of the suit. Partner can bid hearts if I pass, and since I expect to score at least 100 points if we defend against Two Diamonds undoubled, a pass must be judged better than Two Spades or Two Hearts. I think it would be unenterprising not to double, however, and I mark the alternatives:

Double 10
Pass 6
Two Spades 4
Two Hearts 2

Reflections on the Bidding

This situation arose in a Gold Cup final and the double brought in no less than 800 points! North had Q 10 x of diamonds over the dummy's J x x and declarer lost a trick in the play because he did not expect the trumps to be 3-3.

I seldom recommend doubles at a low level without a trump trick, but this was an occasion where it was possible to arrive at a full and satisfactory answer to the important question, "How will the play go?"

17. Often in Danger

In match play, with neither side vulnerable, I hold in third position:

♠ 10 8 5　♡ A J 7 6　◇ J　♣ A 9 7 5 3

My partner, sitting North, opens **One Spade,** East passes, and I respond **Two Clubs.** West intervenes with **Two Hearts** and this is passed to me. The bidding has gone:

South	West	North	East
—	—	1♠	Pass
2♣	2♡	Pass	Pass
?			

The Alternatives

The main choice lies between doubling the hearts and supporting the spades. If I decide to support the spades there may be a question whether I should raise to Two or to Three.

If I had held a doubleton spade and J x of diamonds, I might have chosen 2NT to make some use of my heart honors, but with three spades and a singleton diamond that would be somewhat eccentric. I don't think we need look further than the three alternatives mentioned above:

Three Spades
Two Spades
Double

The Choice

On the surface, all I know about partner's holding is that he has opened One Spade and did not deem his hand worthy of a free rebid over Two Hearts. He is no doubt short of hearts and cannot have much in the way of club support.

There is no bar in our system to opening bids on a four-card major, but there is a strong inference here that partner has five spades. For one thing, he must have been prepared for a Two Heart response, and over that his rebid would presumably have been Two Spades. Another way of arriving at the same conclusion is to reflect that he probably holds nine cards in spades and diamonds.

Two Spades or Three Spades?

If West had passed and North had rebid his spades, I would have had a *very* sound raise to Three Spades. That is sufficient to establish that Two Spades would be an underbid now and that I am worth Three despite holding only three trumps.

What Are the Prospects of a Double?

Certainly we will not make 500; however, if even 300 were likely, it would not be wrong to go for that in preference to an uncertain game.

Many players regularly double in this sort of position, observing rather loosely, "Partner can take it out if he doesn't like it." Even on that basis the double here is much too close for my liking. I see the following objections to it in principle:

(1) I have support for my partner's suit, which I have not shown. If partner has only five spades he will expect them to produce tricks in defence, and they may not.

(2) I don't see a clear-cut line of defence. Partner may well start off with an unfortunate lead such as Queen of clubs from Q x.

(3) My hand does not hold any unpleasant surprise for the declarer. He knows he is missing A J of hearts and was prepared to find them on the wrong side as well. As to my singleton diamond, that may well be duplicated by honors in partner's hand. If declarer's diamonds are something like A x x he will be counting on two losers in any event.

(4) This is not the sort of situation that can turn up in a pairs tournament where one has to make a close double because there is no other way of obtaining a fair result. Probably we *can* beat Two Hearts by one trick but we can score 140 or 170 with much less strain in Two Spades.

However, as I have said, I consider the hand worth Three Spades, and I mark the alternatives:

Three Spades. 10
Two Spades. 5
Double 2

64

Reflections on the Bidding

When partner has been freed from the obligation to rebid, it is often helpful to reflect on what he would have called if there had been no intervention. Here, that line of thought led clearly to the conclusion that he must have intended to rebid his spades.

Of the arguments advanced against a double of Two Hearts, that of paragraph (3) is the one that "busy" players constantly overlook. It is a form of arrogance to double an opponent who has come in freely without taking into account that the bid presumably appeared sound to him when he made it.

I speak with some feeling on this matter, because the fortunes of my team have been endangered on countless occasions by unsuccessful doubles of part-score contracts at the other table. The apologia usually begins along these lines: "How could I tell that the spades would be 5-0?" Or, still more infuriating, "The double was all right. If I had opened a diamond and my partner had underled his Ace of hearts . . ." Idiotic remark! If it needed a tough defence to beat them, the double was *not* all right!

18. The Right Conditions

In a match-pointed pairs tournament, with neither side vulnerable, I hold as dealer:

♠ A K 7 3 2   ♡ J 10 5   ◇ Q 6   ♣ 10 6 4

This is not the sort of hand on which I like to open, whether vulnerable or not, so I pass. West passes and my partner opens **One Diamond**. I respond **One Spade** and now West comes in with **Two Clubs**. This is passed to me and I have to contest in some way after the sequence:

South	West	North	East
Pass	Pass	1◇	Pass
1♠	2♣	Pass	Pass
?			

The Alternatives

There does not seem much likelihood of game at the moment, but I can compete for the part score with either Two Spades or Two Diamonds. As we seem to have the majority of the high cards, we might get a good result from doubling Two Clubs. Any jump bid on my hand would be excessive in view of partner's pass on the second round, so the alternatives are:

Two Spades
Two Diamonds
Double

The Choice

If partner has a genuine opening we should be able to make at least eight tricks or so in spades or diamonds, and if he is a bit light in high cards, he will have a fair diamond suit and we can probably make Two Diamonds.

Two Spades would score better than Two Diamonds, but a disadvantage of bidding Two Spades is that we can't go back to diamonds. At worst, partner might hold:

66

(1) ♠ x ♡ K x x x ◇ A J 10 x x ♣ A x x

Now Two Spades could play very awkwardly.

On the other hand, if I bid Two Diamonds, we can still play in Two Spades. With the match-point situation in mind, partner will bid Two Spades not only when he has three spades and four diamonds, but also with:

(2) ♠ 10 x x ♡ A Q x ◇ A J x x x ♣ x x

A Double Co-operative

Two Diamonds, then, is more flexible than Two Spades, but a double leaves the widest choice of all. I have less in clubs than I would like but my hand is nevertheless maximum in defensive values, considering that I passed originally. West also passed to begin with, and his hand is likely to consist of A Q J or K Q J six times in clubs with perhaps a side King and 6-4-2-1 or 6-3-3-1 distribution. He will expect to find something in the dummy, but may be disappointed. Or rather, he will be disappointed if my partner has the sort of hand on which he can pass the double.

Partner will not assume that my double, made in front of the club bidder, is based on strong trumps. Clearly he will be happy to pass on hand (1) above. On hand (2) he will remove to Two Spades. He will accept the double only when he has fair defensive values and not more than two spades.

It is true that one down doubled will not be as good as making Two Spades or Three Diamonds, but the difference will be small, and these doubles often bring in 300. I mark the alternatives:

Double 10
Two Diamonds 6
Two Spades 5

Reflections on the Bidding

On most occasions in this book I bear down on marginal doubles in the part-score area, so I include this example to show that I don't object to a snap double when the conditions are right. These are factors that make the double sound policy:

67

Partner will know that the double is not based primarily on trump tricks, for I am under the bidder and West must have a good suit.

If he doesn't like the double, he will have no problem about taking it out. He has the choice of Two Spades or Two Diamonds, and possibly even Two Hearts.

If he does pass the double, he will presumably lead a spade and the defence will be off on the right foot.

19. A Keener Edge

My opponents are vulnerable in a pairs event and as dealer I hold:

♠ A K Q 10 3   ♡ 5   ◇ A 10 4   ♣ K J 8 2

This does not qualify for a Two bid in our system, so I open **One Spade.** West overcalls with a jump to **Three Hearts,** my partner passes, and East bids **Four Hearts.** I have to make my next call at an inconvenient level after the sequence:

South	West	North	East
1♠	3♡	Pass	4♡
?			

The Alternatives

I can take my chance in defence, either passing or doubling. I can also contest in one of two ways, bidding either Four Spades or 4NT asking partner to choose a minor suit. Thus the alternatives are:

4NT
Four Spades
Double
Pass

The Choice

The first question is, as always, "Who is likely, on the evidence so far, to make what?"

In spades I have six more or less certain tricks in my own hand and conceivably I might make no more. Four Spades would then go down the fatal 700—more than their vulnerable game is worth. But that would be a gloomy view to take and I am going to judge the hand on the assumption that a sacrifice in Four Spades would show a profit as against a game for the other side.

Whether they can in fact make Four Hearts is difficult to judge. All I can say is that my hand seems to contain fair defensive possibilities.

Match-Point Considerations

At rubber bridge I wouldn't think of sacrificing, nor would there be any particular reason to double. At match points one has to press this kind of decision to a keener edge. If we can beat Four Hearts it may be important that we double and score 200, for other pairs may be making 110 or 140 in spades. If Four Hearts is on, it is essential that we sacrifice. To let them play in Four Hearts undoubled would be to accept a second-best result either way, and at match points that is seldom right.

A Double Co-operative

Fortunately, I am not forced to make the difficult guess as to whether they will make Four Hearts. I can call on partner's assistance by doubling. Why should partner take the double to be anything other than a penalty double? One reason is that I cannot be doubling on trump strength, a second that I must have length in spades, for with a strong hand containing only four spades and short hearts the opening bid would be different. Particularly at this vulnerability, the double says to partner, "The bidding has gone high but I am not prepared to surrender. I have enough spades to think that if we cannot beat Four Hearts, we can sacrifice profitably. If you are short in spades we can defend, but if you have three spades and no useful defensive value, I want you to bid Four Spades."

Summing Up

On this basis a double is obviously the best call. While partner will normally choose between passing and bidding Four Spades, he can also take out into a six-card minor suit. That is one reason why 4NT, forcing partner to select a minor, would be quite wrong. The other reason is that we expect to go down not more than 500 points in Four Spades, while if partner were forced to bid Five Diamonds on a weak suit, the penalty could be beyond the safety mark.

As between a pass and a unilateral sacrifice, a pass is better because a sacrifice costing 300, even if it saves the game, will still be a bad result if Four Hearts is not bid at some tables. So I mark the alternatives:

```
Double . . . . . . . . . . . . . . . . . . . . . 10
Pass . . . . . . . . . . . . . . . . . . . . . . .  6
Four Spades . . . . . . . . . . . . . . . . .  4
4NT  . . . . . . . . . . . . . . . . . . . . . .  1
```

Reflections on the Bidding

A remark in the final paragraph above draws attention to an aspect of match-point tactics that is seldom regarded.

In view of the strength of South's hand, it seems at least possible that opponents have stretched a bit and that Four Hearts will not be bid at some tables. Let's take that to extremes and assume that yours is the only table at which East-West have bid up to Four Hearts. Now if the contract can be defeated, obviously you don't want to sacrifice. If it can be made, and no one else is in it, you will score a bottom whether you lose 620 or 300 in a sacrifice. So your only chance of a good score is to hope that they have overreached themselves.

The principle is that when opponents in a pairs event seem to have bid their cards to the limit, you must not sacrifice. That applies particularly to slam contracts at equal vulnerability. Say that opponents reach Six Hearts not vulnerable and you save judiciously in Six Spades. You find that the slam could have been made and are well pleased with your loss of 500—until you open the scoresheet and find that every other pair your way has lost only 450 or 480, so you still get a bottom score. Next time, just hope that you can set them.

PART THREE

Tactical Moves

In this section, various tactical manoeuvres are discussed. Among them are ways of escaping from a threatening penalty double, preparing a defence in a competitive auction, placing the bid in the right hand, extensions of the lead-directing double, and tactical underbids in certain sequences.

20. Lines of Retreat

At rubber bridge my side is a game ahead when I pick up in third position:

♠ 4   ♡ Q 7 3   ◇ J 8 7 5 2   ♣ 10 6 4 3

My partner opens **One Spade,** East passes, and I have no two thoughts about doing likewise. West reopens with a **double,** my partner passes, and so does East. I have to decide whether to start any rescue operations after the sequence:

South	West	North	East
—	—	1♠	Pass
Pass	Double	Pass	Pass
?			

The Alternatives

There are four ways of attempting to improve the situation. I can redouble, bid 1NT, or take out into one of the minor suits. It could also be right to let the double stand, so the alternatives are:

Two Diamonds
Two Clubs
1NT
Redouble
Pass

The Choice

Partners who open One Spade on a hand that is not particularly strong usually have a five-card suit. Also, had North been weak in spades he could have bid 1NT after West's double, with the intention, if necessary, of redoubling for a rescue. Thus, I don't expect to find him

73

with a suit like A K x x. However, he could hold a fair five-card suit and still have a very awkward journey. A pass could not be criticized, but I am playing for points, not praise, and my instinct is to look for a more promising contract.

If the choice were between passing and rescuing into one of the minors, I would pass, but better techniques are available. Thus, 1NT would inform partner that I disliked the notion of One Spade doubled and held scattered strength in the other suits. I wouldn't classify this necessarily as an "unusual no trump" showing length in the minors, but if partner had four cards in either minor he would surely take out 1NT.

Tactical Advantage of Redouble

A redouble would surely be S.O.S., because I passed originally and also because if I were satisfied with the double of One Spade I would leave it in.

Like 1NT, redouble gives us the chance to play in a second suit of partner's choosing, and it has the important advantage that it makes it possible to play 1NT from partner's side, without the prospect of a spade lead through the strength. A further point, perhaps a small one, is that if partner happens to be strong he can pass the redouble and let East do the worrying. By redoubling I at least prevent partner from saying afterwards: "Why couldn't you leave it in? I had seven (eight, nine?) tricks in my own hand . . ."

The Minor Suits

To rescue directly into either minor suit would be a mistake—if only because we would by-pass 1NT. Also, we could end in the wrong suit. To select Two Diamonds might be calamitous. Two Clubs is slightly better, because if it is firmly doubled a retreat to diamonds is still possible.

The arguments for a redouble put it clearly ahead of the other forms of rescue, and I mark the alternatives:

Redouble 10
Pass......................... 7
1NT 6
Two Clubs.................. 3
Two Diamonds 1

Reflections on the Bidding

Two Diamonds was the worst, and redouble the best, of the rescue manoeuvres because Two Diamonds left open the fewest lines of retreat, redouble the greatest number. That is a line of thought worth bearing in mind for many situations where the future seems hazardous or obscure.

21. Powerful Transmission

My partner at rubber bridge is an experienced tournament player. Second to speak in the final game, I am sorting my cards with pleasurable amazement when the opponent on my right opens **One Heart.** My hand is:

♠ A Q 6 4   ♡ K J   ◇ A K Q   ♣ A Q 5 2

So much for my intended Two Club opening! There are now three possible overcalls—2NT, double and Two Hearts. The objection to 2NT is that the best chance for game is to find partner with a few spades, and almost surely he will be unable to bid at all over 2NT. I can bid Two Hearts, but he may take that as game-forcing and we have no guarantee of game. The safest course seems to be to **double.** West passes, my partner responds Two Diamonds, and the opener passes. That gives me a further problem after the sequence:

South	West	North	East
—	—	—	1♡
Double	Pass	2◇	Pass
?			

The Alternatives

It is difficult to obtain intelligent co-operation from a partner who cannot have more than a Queen or two Jacks, and a case can be made for such extremes as a pass or Five Diamonds, as well as for intermediate bids in that suit. Two Hearts, if interpreted as a force and not a heart suit, might be a good move. Both 2NT and 3NT would have their supporters. It makes a long list:

> Five Diamonds
> Four Diamonds
> Three Diamonds
> 3NT
> 2NT
> Two Hearts
> Pass

The Choice

Despite the slight risk, I see now that I ought to have overcalled with Two Hearts on the previous round. Over a response of Three Diamonds I would raise to Four and he would have a better picture of my strength than I can give him now without plunging into game.

However, I have to deal with the situation as it stands. First I must judge if there is a reasonable chance of game in any contract and, if so, is there any sensible way of getting there?

Diamonds a Better Prospect than No Trump

Not much experience is needed to appreciate that game at no trump is improbable. The natural assumption is that the vulnerable opener has five or six hearts headed by the Ace or A Q, together with both the black Kings. After a heart lead and continuation there would be nowhere to go. It might not even help if partner had Q x x of hearts, for by beginning with Ace and another heart (and in other ways) the defence could immobilize the dummy.

Diamonds offer a better chance because then there will at least be some entry cards to partner's hand. It is not certain that he has five diamonds, but it is more than likely, for on a very weak hand he would choose as low a call as possible in response to the double. There would be a play for Five Diamonds if he held either of these hands:

(1) ♠ x x   ♡ x x   ◇ 10 x x x x x   ♣ 10 x x

(2) ♠ J x x   ♡ x x x   ◇ J x x x x   ♣ x x

Thus, one of our original questions is answered: Game is not out of the question. Whether there is a sensible way of getting there is another matter!

Four Diamonds May Not Be Enough

Three Diamonds would be harmless but meaningless, for partner would never be able to advance.

Four Diamonds would be a strong call but I doubt whether he would go to Five on either of the two hands shown above. If they were a little stronger in distribution, yes.

Four Diamonds is the best game try we have found, and the remaining hope lies in Two Hearts.

What Would Two Hearts Mean?

According to most text-books, to double a contract and bid the suit on the next round means that one wants to play in the suit. In tournament play, the bid is more often used to extract a further call from partner, and that is how I think my present partner would interpret it. The weakness of his hand, together with his holding in hearts, should remove any doubt.

His first reaction to Two Hearts will be that I am asking for another suit or for a partial guard in hearts. He will probably bid a strangled Two Spades on x x x or 2NT with four small hearts. In either case I can follow with Four Diamonds and I think he will get the message that I was too strong for a direct raise to Four. That may encourage him to bid Five on hands (1) and (2) above. If so, this is the best solution.

Summing Up

The only bid we have not discussed is a direct Five Diamonds. If one is going to gamble, that is a better proposition than 3NT, but if by chance partner had only four diamonds it could go astray. On the basis that Two Hearts is a temporary force which will be followed up with Four Diamonds, I mark the alternatives:

Two Hearts	10
Four Diamonds	8
Five Diamonds	7
Three Diamonds	4
Pass	4
2NT	2
3NT	1

Reflections on the Bidding

Two points of partnership understanding arise from this hand. One concerns the immediate overcall in the opponent's suit. In the early days of contract this was played as game-forcing, and the tradition remains for many players. I am sure it is better to make the overcall on any strong hand not well suited to a double and to treat it as forcing for two rounds only—the response and the rebid.

The other technical point is the interpretation of Two Hearts by South after he has doubled One Heart on the previous round. In American tournament circles this bid has for a long while been played as a sort of follow-up to the double, asking partner to describe his hand further. That idea has been adopted in Britain by most duplicate players.

22. Out of Fashion

At rubber bridge both sides are vulnerable, and as dealer I pick up:

♠ A K 10 7 6 2   ♡ 4   ◇ K Q 9 6 3   ♣ 5

I open **One Spade** and West overcalls with **Two Hearts.** My partner raises to **Two Spades** and East bids **Three Hearts.** I am faced with a familiar tactical problem after the sequence:

South	West	North	East
1♠	2♡	2♠	3♡
?			

The Alternatives

I can jump directly to Four Spades or approach that end more deviously by way of Three Spades or even a pass. Four Diamonds must also be considered. Thus, the alternatives are:

Four Spades
Three Spades
Four Diamonds
Pass

The Choice

My objective is clear enough: I want to play in Four Spades, which I can probably make. I do not want to contend with Five Hearts if I can help it.

It is usual to suppress the second suit in this situation and to employ one of three well-known stratagems. There is something to be said for each of them.

Four Spades

This is the straightforward call and it has the merit of raising the auction to a level at which it may be difficult for either opponent to overcall.

Three Spades

The object of this tactical underbid is to persuade the opponents that you are stretching when later you go to Four Spades over Four Hearts, assuming that the opportunity arises. The stratagem is well known and a further disadvantage—as compared with Four Spades—is that the opponents have more room in which to assess their potentialities. Moreover, opponents will sometimes refrain from disturbing Three Spades because they are fearful of having to compete against Four Spades.

Pass

This is a more subtle way of achieving the same kind of result, but it also requires more nerve. I shall look foolish if the opponents buy the contract for Three Hearts when we have eleven tricks in spades! However, since I have only 12 points, the odds are that someone else will bid. Either West will go to Four Hearts or my partner will persist with Three Spades. In either case, my eventual bid of Four Spades will be underestimated and may even be doubled.

Four Diamonds

There remains the unfashionable call of Four Diamonds. The advantage of exposing my two-suiter to all who choose to believe in it is that I go far to solving the problem that may arise at the level of Five.

Suppose that we get to Four Spades by fast or slow stages and that the opponents inconveniently persist to Five Hearts. Even if partner doubles in front of me I shall be tempted to go to Five Spades. I shall not have to make this guess if I have bid Four Diamonds on the way. As an example, compare these two hands for partner:

(1) ♠ J 9 x x　♡ x x　♢ A J x x　♣ J 10 x

(2) ♠ Q 9 x x　♡ x x x　♢ x x　♣ K Q 10 x

On hand (1) he will go to Five Spades and on (2) he will double. Either way, I shall be content to let him decide.

Summing Up

I would admire anyone who had the nerve to pass, but since the object of the problem is to point out the merit of Four Diamonds I mark the alternatives:

Four Diamonds...............10
Pass........................ 8
Four Spades................. 6
Three Spades................ 4

Reflections on the Bidding

I think there is a general tendency to overlook the advantage of bidding second suits during a competitive auction. Suppose that South holds:

♠ x ♡ K Q J x x x ◇ x x ♣ A Q J x

The bidding goes:

South	West	North	East
1♡	1♠	3♡	3♠
?			

Now what is wrong with bidding Four Clubs? It will stop a club lead, you say, against Four Hearts? But you weren't expecting that anyway! What it *will* do is help your partner make an intelligent decision if they go to Four Spades.

23. Directional Asking Bid

With neither side vulnerable in a team event I hold as dealer:

♠ A 3   ♡ Q J 7 5 4   ◇ A 10 6 2   ♣ K 3

I open **One Heart** and my partner responds **Two Clubs.** I am a point or two short for 2NT now and **Two Diamonds** is better than Two Hearts. At this point West, who passed on the previous round, comes in with **Two Spades.** My partner bids **Three Spades** and East **doubles.** This calls for some study, the bidding having gone:

South	West	North	East
1♡	Pass	2♣	Pass
2◇	2♠	3♠	Double
?			

The Alternatives

Partner may be interested in my spade guard, which I could show by bidding 3NT or by redoubling. Perhaps, on the other hand, he is confirming diamonds and is thinking of a slam. In that case it might help to show my club control by bidding Four Clubs. It could hardly be a good idea to bid Four Spades at this moment, for that can come on the next round if partner supports diamonds. As the situation is obscure, I can pass and see what partner will do after the double. That makes four alternatives:

Four Clubs
3NT
Redouble
Pass

The Choice

Partner's bid of Three Spades, the enemy suit, can have one of two purposes. He may be attempting to steer us into 3NT if I have a guard in spades, or he may be signalling support for diamonds and slam intentions.

The sort of hand on which he would bid Three Spades as a directional asking bid is:

(1) ♠ Q x   ♡ x x   ◇ K J x   ♣ A Q x x x x
Or:
(2) ♠ J 9 x   ♡ K x   ◇ K x x   ♣ A J 10 x x

Alternatively, he might bid Three Spades to signify strong support for diamonds on a wide variety of hands. This would be an example:

♠ x   ♡ A x   ◇ K J x x   ♣ A 10 x x x x

Four Clubs Could Be a Mistake

If partner has the first type of hand we do not want to go beyond 3NT. Four Clubs could therefore be a mistake. If partner is looking toward a high contract in diamonds, his next bid will reveal the fact and then I can think about showing my controls.

A Pass Not Helpful

For the moment I must assume that his bid of Three spades is a suggestion for 3NT. If so, it will not help him if I pass now. He will assume that I have no stop in spades and will abandon the idea of playing at no trump.

Who Has the King of Spades?

That is the critical question; its answer determines whether I bid 3NT or redouble. If partner's spades are Q x as in hand (1), I want him to play 3NT if East has the spade King. On the whole, I think that is more likely because East's double of Three Spades, if it meant anything, was an indication to his partner that spades would be a safe lead. Moreover, West's delayed entry into the bidding could well be explained by a holding such as:

♠ J 10 9 x x x   ♡ A 10 9 x   ◇ x x   ♣ x

One further point is that a redouble suggests the Ace of spades rather than a secondary stop such as K J x. It answers the immediate problem of keeping the bidding under 3NT, it assists us to play 3NT from the right side, and it maintains interest in any forward move. That makes it a good call, and I mark the alternatives:

Redouble .10
3NT 7
Four Clubs. 3
Pass. 3

Reflections on the Bidding

The hand is a good example of the so-called directional asking bid and of the way to respond to it. This technique was devised by the inventors of the Baron system and has been used by British tournament players for over twenty years.

24. Uncertain Sacrifice

In a team event the opponents are vulnerable, we are not. My partner deals and passes, the second player passes, and my hand is:

♠ 10 5 2   ♡ 8 3   ◇ A K 7 6 2   ♣ 6 4 3

There is not a lot to be gained by a semi-psychic opening in a minor suit, so I pass. West opens with **One Heart,** my partner overcalls with **One Spade,** and East raises to **Two Hearts.** I have a chance to enter the bidding at a safe level after the sequence:

South	West	North	East
—	—	Pass	Pass
Pass	1♡	1♠	2♡
?			

The Alternatives

The values are there for a raise to Two Spades. On tactical grounds a case can be made for Three Diamonds and also for a pass. Anything else would be peculiar, so the alternatives are:

> Three Diamonds
> Two Spades
> Pass

The Choice

Whether the opponents can make a game in hearts I can't judge at this moment, but they must be fairly close. My partner passed originally although he had a biddable spade suit, so he won't have any more in defence than I have. Still, two tricks from each of us would be enough and I am not going to start from the assumption that Four Hearts will necessarily make.

That is why I am not happy about bidding Two Spades, which is what my hand is worth. I don't want to give partner the idea that I am looking toward a sacrifice. Suppose he holds something like:

♠ A x x x x x   ♡ x x   ◇ x x   ♣ K 10 x

Once the spades have been supported he may sacrifice over Four Hearts in a doubtful cause.

I would rather pass than support spades at this point. We are surely out-gunned on the deal.

The other possibility, Three Diamonds, has the obvious advantage of suggesting a good lead if we eventually defend. Moreover, it should help partner to judge how high to go in spades. He will realize that I am showing high cards in diamonds, for with a long suit I would have pre-empted on the first round at this vulnerability.

Would Three Diamonds Be Too Dangerous?

Seven tricks may be our limit in either spades or diamonds, so in theory there is a risk of losing 300 on a part-score deal. However, it is not at all likely that they will catch us. First, they will have to double Three Diamonds, and after that, Three Spades. As the bidding has gone, neither opponent is likely to be strong in spades. I just don't see their doubling us at the Three level.

All the tactical advantages are with Three Diamonds, and the bid is not so risky as it seems. I mark the alternatives:

> Three Diamonds..............10
> Pass........................ 6
> Two Spades.................. 4

Reflections on the Bidding

This was a slightly deceptive problem, because Three Diamonds is the sort of bid that a good player usually does not make. A raise to Two Spades would often be the right response to partner's overcall. Here, however, there was a strong objection to it on tactical grounds.

When it is plain that opponents have the balance of the cards, it is important to ask yourself, "Do I want to encourage my partner to sacrifice?" If not, it is usually better to pass even though you have the values for a raise. There was a hand in one of Britain's matches during the Olympiad at Turin when with both sides vulnerable South held:

♠ Q x x   ♡ 9 8 x x   ◇ 10 x   ♣ K J x x

87

The bidding began:

South	West	North	East
—	—	—	Pass
Pass	2♠	3♡	3♠
?			

South bid Four Hearts, which was safe enough for the moment, for the Two Spade opening was not a strong bid in the opponents' system. However, the sequel was that North, with a red two-suiter, went to Five Hearts over Four Spades and lost 800, sacrificing against a contract that might not have been made.

On this occasion South was too weak offensively to suggest a sacrifice when opponents had the higher ranking suit. In the example we have been looking at, the fault with Two Spades was that South's defensive prospects were too good for him to propose a sacrifice until partner had the message about the diamonds.

25. Minority Vote

Playing in a pairs event against opponents of average standard, I hold as dealer:

♠ A 3   ♡ A 9 8 6 5 4   ◇ 7   ♣ A 6 3 2

Both sides are vulnerable and I open **One Heart.** West overcalls with **One Spade** and my partner raises to **Two Hearts.** East now comes in with **Three Diamonds** and I have a problem in tactics after the sequence:

South	West	North	East
1♡	1♠	2♡	3◇
?			

The Alternatives

Three Hearts or Four Hearts would be straightforward. Among the tactical possibilities are Four Diamonds, Four Clubs, and a pass. If we consider nothing more eccentric than these, the alternatives are:

Four Hearts
Three Hearts
Four Diamonds
Four Clubs
Pass

The Choice

We must have a play for Four Hearts and, unless partner is trickless, we should have a defence against Four Spades. Thus, the general objective is to play in Four Hearts or, if they defend, to extract the maximum penalty.

Not the Moment for an Underbid

I don't see this as a borderline competitive hand on which we might make Four Hearts and they Four Spades. On hands like that (as we noted in example 22) it may be good tactics to underbid, partly to deceive the opponents and partly to judge more accurately where the balance of strength lies. Here, they have so far not even agreed on spades, and if I jump to the level of Four they may not get together—assuming, that is, that they have a fit at all. If I pass or bid just Three Hearts, I give West the opportunity to rebid spades and East will probably be able to go to Four Spades.

Preparing a Defence

The best way, then, to attain our first objective—being allowed to play in Four Hearts—is to bid at the Four level. The second objective is to prepare the best defence against Four Spades. That means taking our ruff in diamonds. If partner leads a heart against Four Spades doubled I can win with the Ace (I hope) and return my diamond, but there may be no subsequent entry to his hand that will enable him to give me the diamond ruff.

One possibility is to bid Four Clubs. Then I can take the club lead, return a diamond, and perhaps later put partner in with the King of hearts.

But why not Four Diamonds ? That looks better still. For one thing, partner's entry may be in clubs, not hearts. For another, releasing the Ace of clubs may make it possible for West to discard a diamond on dummy's clubs.

When I win the first round of trumps, it shouldn't be difficult to decide where partner's entry lies. He may think of making a suit preference signal when he makes the opening lead of a diamond. If he does not, and I cannot see from the table which suit to return, I can lay down the Ace of clubs and note whether he gives me an encouraging signal.

I don't see any disadvantage in the Four Diamond call. A partner who has raised to Two Hearts and probably lacks an Ace is unlikely to carry me beyond Four Hearts. It fits in with both the original plans and I mark the alternatives:

$$
\begin{array}{lr}
\text{Four Diamonds} & 10 \\
\text{Four Clubs} & 7 \\
\text{Four Hearts} & 6 \\
\text{Three Hearts} & 3 \\
\text{Pass} & 3 \\
\end{array}
$$

Reflections on the Bidding

In the original deal from which this problem was taken, North-South had to score the diamond ruff to defeat Four Spades by just one trick. The problem was set in the *Bridge World* and editor Alphonse Moyse, Jr., castigated his expert panel when only one out of fifty-eight voted for Four Diamonds. A few mentioned the bid but did not follow it up. I don't know why. It seems to me a good bid which I would be satisfied to find at the table.

26. A Possible Extension

In a pairs event the opponents are playing a Two Club system in which Aces are shown immediately in response to a Two Club opening. They are vulnerable and in fourth position I hold:

♠ 7 5   ♡ K 10 9 6 2   ◇ 3   ♣ J 10 7 4 2

West, on my left, opens **Two Clubs** and my partner **doubles.** That sort of double is sometimes used to show strength in clubs, but that is ruled out by my holding here, and I assume that the double is for a take-out. East passes and I respond **Two Hearts.** West bids **Two Spades,** partner raises to **Three Hearts,** and East bids **Four Spades.** The hand is probably going to end in a sacrifice and, while I might anticipate with a jump to Six Hearts, I think it is just as good to see what develops after **Five Hearts.** As expected, West jumps to **Six Spades.** That is followed by two passes and I am left to make the final decision after the sequence:

South	West	North	East
—	2♣	Double	Pass
2♡	2♠	3♡	4♠
5♡	6♠	Pass	Pass
?			

The Alternatives

I have to decide in principle between sacrificing and defending. The obvious bid, if I am going to sacrifice, is Seven Hearts, but an argument could be advanced for bidding Seven Diamonds first. Similarly, while I would be content if we could beat them undoubled, there might be a tactical reason for doubling. If we include those less likely calls, the alternatives are:

Seven Hearts
Seven Diamonds
Double
Pass

The Choice

A take-out double of a Two Club opening is uncommon, but players who use Ace responses often open Two Clubs on distributional hands. My partner may have quite a good hand—no doubt with a shortage in spades.

Can West Be Bluffing?

That is always a possibility in this vulnerability situation. West may think that by jumping to Six Spades he can stampede us into a sacrifice. Somehow I don't think that's the situation here. Our bidding has not sounded particularly weak, and West can scarcely be sure that we intend to sacrifice.

What Are Our Chances in Defence?

Difficult to estimate. Partner has left the decision to me, and my defensive prospects are of an uncertain nature. They consist of the singleton diamond (partner may hold the Ace or may have length) and the clubs, such as they are. If my partner held the Ace of diamonds, would he lead it if I doubled? No, it's too far-fetched. It is doubtful whether he would regard a double as lead-directing at all.

If We Sacrifice, Will That Be a Good Score?

That may depend on whether we lose 500 or 700 in Six Hearts. The slam won't be bid at some tables, I dare say, and then North-South will lose 650 or 680. If Seven Hearts is going to cost 700 we may as well take our chance in defence. Actually, I am hopeful that we shall make about ten tricks in hearts. We should have a good fit. If we lose 500 that may not be too bad even if the slam could have been defeated, because at some tables our side may not get into the bidding at all.

Little Danger of Seven Spades

I have made up my mind to sacrifice and the only question that remains is whether I should bid Seven Diamonds on the way. The only point in that would be to suggest to the opponents that I was void in diamonds and was indicating a lead in case we had to defend against Seven Spades. Sometimes that manoeuvre is worth considering, but here it is unlikely that they will bid Seven or that they will make it.

Seven Diamonds would be pointless, therefore, but also harmless in the sense that no doubt we are destined to play in Seven Hearts doubled. On the understanding that the credit for Seven Diamonds is unearned, I mark the alternatives:

Seven Hearts	10
Seven Diamonds	8
Pass	4
Double	2

Reflections on the Bidding

An important consideration here was whether the sacrifice was likely to cost 500 or 700. We observed a similar situation when discussing example 19.

Two unlikely stratagems were rejected which might, nevertheless, be remembered for another occasion. There was the suggestion that South might double Six Spades on the strength of his singleton diamond. The Lightner lead-directing double usually denotes a void but the idea can sometimes be extended to singletons. Of course there must be a reasonable expectation that partner will have the critical Ace and will think of leading it.

The other idea was that if South was afraid of driving the opponents to Seven Spades, he should bid Seven Diamonds as though indicating a sure lead against the grand slam. Plainly that was not necessary here. The opportunity for such a manoeuvre occurs more often when the opponents have not exhausted themselves. Say the enemy suit is spades and you decide you will have to sacrifice if they go to Six. By making some imaginary cue-bid at the Five level you may succeed in creating the impression, or at least the suspicion, that you possess an unexpected void!

27. A Practical Illustration

In a team event my partner, North, is the dealer and our opponents are vulnerable. My hand is:

♠ Q J 9 3 2   ♡ —   ◇ J 10 4 2   ♣ 8 6 5 3

North opens **One Diamond** and East, on my right, overcalls with **One Heart**. What action, if any, am I to take after the sequence:

South	West	North	East
—	—	1◇	1♡
?			

The Alternatives

Even for players who like their free bids to be well up to standard, this should be seen as a problem of tactics. One can pass, certainly, whatever one's view about free bids. One Spade and Two Diamonds are obvious possibilities. Some players would make this an occasion for a psychic foray, such as 1NT or double, but I propose to stay with the more serious alternatives, namely:

> Two Diamonds
> One Spade
> Pass

The Choice

The best way to approach this may be to examine the arguments for and against each of the three calls.

Two Diamonds

The case for: If we make this limited bid on the first round we are better placed later to contest with Four Spades, should that seem advisable. Partner will appreciate, from the failure to bid One Spade on the first round, that we have this defenceless type of hand.

The case against: Only that the plan to bid Two Diamonds now and Four Spades later may cut across partner's intentions. North may have good defence against hearts.

One Spade

The case for: This may be the last safe opportunity to introduce the spade suit into what will surely be a competitive auction. If partner cannot support spades, it may be better to let opponents play than to press on high in diamonds.

The case against: If you bid One Spade now and support diamonds at a high level on the next round you will give partner a false impression of your defensive strength. Then you will not know what to do when he doubles Four Hearts. Or Four Hearts may be doubled before you have shown your diamond support, and then again your action will be a guess.

Pass

The case for: If we hold our peace now we shall hear the natural reactions of West and North to the bid of One Heart. Then we shall be able to judge better whether or not to defend in diamonds. That we shall not have a chance to mention spades as well is unimportant, because the hand is sure to produce one more trick in diamonds than in spades. A further point is that by bidding on what are probably the weaker hands, our side may help the opposition to judge one another's shortages.

The case against: The point about the unimportance of showing the spades is conceded, and so is that about helping the opponents by talking too much. Whether the decision on later rounds will be easier if South passes now is more doubtful.

Summing Up

The case against One Spade is certainly stronger than any that can be made against the other calls. Two Diamonds could not be criticized, but the arguments for a pass impress me. I mark the alternatives:

Pass.........................10
Two Diamonds 8
One Spade 4

Reflections on the Bidding

When this problem, with one small difference, was put to a panel, Two Diamonds won the majority of votes—though the argument for a pass was noted. By a coincidence, an almost identical decision confronted an American player during a match against Britain in the Olympiad at Turin two years later. With neither side vulnerable South held:

♠ Q 8 7 5 2   ♡ —   ◇ J 9 7 5 4   ♣ Q 3 2

The bidding began:

South	West	North	East
Pass	Pass	1◇	1♡
1♠			

When the auction next came around to South the opponents were in Four Hearts. Having concealed his diamond support, South bid Five Diamonds. This was doubled by one opponent and taken back to Five Hearts by the other. Now North doubled, everyone passed, and Five Hearts was made. Had South passed or bid Two Diamonds on the first round, no doubt his side would have judged the hand better and sacrificed all the way up to Six Diamonds.

28. A Little Rope

In a pairs event, with neither side vulnerable, my partner opens **One Diamond** and the next player passes. My hand is:

♠ K J 9 6 2   ♡ —   ◇ 9 7 5   ♣ K 10 8 6 2

I respond **One Spade** and, after a pass by West, partner rebids **Two Diamonds**. East passes, and I have a rebid problem after the sequence:

South	West	North	East
—	—	1◇	Pass
1♠	Pass	2◇	Pass
?			

The Alternatives

A pass of Two Diamonds is a possibility and so is a raise to Three. I could repeat the spades or make a forward move in clubs. That makes the alternatives:

Three Diamonds
Three Clubs
Two Spades
Pass

The Choice

The next call has to be considered from two angles: Is the hand worth another bid, in that a pass may lead to a missed game? Even if game is unlikely, is it advisable to make another bid for tactical and defensive reasons?

Is It Likely that We Can Make a Game?

I doubt whether we can make more than nine or ten tricks in diamonds. Since nothing has been heard of the hearts, it is likely that partner has four, but it does not follow that my hand will provide three ruffs. There may be duplication and there may be difficulty with entries. As soon as the defenders come in they will lead a trump, if they have not done so originally.

Game may be on, it is true, if partner has a void or a singleton Ace in one of the black suits. I could bid Three Diamonds without much risk of going too high. That would certainly be a better bid than Two Spades, suggesting a much better suit, or than Three Clubs, which would be forcing and would invite 3NT.

Is It Necessary to Bid for Tactical Reasons?

This is a more important question, because even if I pass Two Diamonds now I shall probably have another chance. Partner's strength is limited by his simple rebid and opponents presumably have nine or ten hearts between them. No doubt West is the stronger hand, for East had a chance to come in over One Diamond. It is highly probable that if I pass Two Diamonds West will reopen with a double or Two Hearts.

Do I really want to prevent that by making a mild pre-empt such as Three Diamonds? I have an idea that if opponents find their fit in hearts they may have cause to regret it! Quite a likely type of hand for partner is:

♠ x   ♡ K Q 9 x   ◇ A Q J x x x   ♣ J x

Two Hearts he will pass, and if they reach Four we will collect a good penalty.

If West bids Two Hearts and partner doubles at once I shall take out into Three Diamonds. If partner bids Three Diamonds himself, over Two Hearts, I will go to Four Diamonds over Three Hearts. Any such development seems satisfactory.

Resorting to *cliché*, this seems a moment where, if allowed a little rope, the opponents may hang themselves. I mark the alternatives:

Pass........................10
Three Diamonds.............. 6
Three Clubs................. 2
Two Spades................. 1

Reflections on the Bidding

The principle that emerges from this hand is that there is no need to prevent opponents from getting together when, if they do so, they will run into bad distribution. It is not when you have a void or a singleton, but when you have x x or x x x, that you may have to take defensive measures.

Suppose that after the same bidding by North-South, One Diamond —One Spade—Two Diamonds, South had held:

♠ A x x x x ♡ x x ◇ K J x ♣ x x x

There won't be a game anywhere and South is not worth a raise on his values, but now there is a tactical case for Three Diamonds.

The same sort of argument applies to opening pre-emptive bids. Compare these two hands:

(1) ♠ x x ♡ A Q J 10 x x x ◇ 10 x x ♣ x

(2) ♠ — ♡ A Q 9 8 x x x ◇ 10 9 8 x x ♣ x

On hand (1) you should pre-empt as high as you dare in relation to vulnerability and position at the table. On hand (2) you can afford to sit back and listen to the others.

PART FOUR

Making Progress After an Intervening Bid

In most of the examples in this section an intervening bid has created a problem. Sometimes the difficulty is simply lack of bidding space, at other times opposition bidding makes the choice of contract a delicate matter.

29. As Opportunity Offers

My partner at rubber bridge plays a sound game without any flights of fancy. I deal and pick up:

♠ A 4   ♡ 7 5 2   ◇ K 8   ♣ A Q 10 7 5 3

Neither side is vulnerable and I open **One Club.** This is doubled on my left, partner **redoubles,** and East passes. If I bid Two Clubs partner will assume that I have a weak opening, so I pass and West bids **One Heart.** Partner bids **Two Clubs** and East passes. The bidding has gone:

South	West	North	East
1♣	Double	Redouble	Pass
Pass	1♡	2♣	Pass
?			

The Alternatives

There could be various opinions about the next move, ranging from a pass to a force of Two Hearts or a gambling 3NT. Three Clubs would be a popular choice and we must also look at Four Clubs and 2NT. The best call should be somewhere among the following:

Four Clubs
Three Clubs
3NT
2NT·
Two Hearts
Pass

The Choice

Partner's general strength can be estimated within fairly close limits. His redouble, in preference to 1NT or a jump in clubs, was an expression of confidence that we hold the balance of the cards. The odds are against his having a heart stop, for with a guarded King or Queen he might have preferred 1NT on the second round. Any of the following hands would be consistent with his bidding:

(1) ♠ Q 10 x   ♡ x x   ◇ A 10 x x   ♣ K x x x

(2) ♠ K x x x   ♡ 10 x x   ◇ A x   ♣ K x x x

(3) ♠ Q x x x   ♡ A x   ◇ Q x   ♣ J 9 x x x

It is clear from these examples that there can be no question of passing on my hand. We would not be far from game on any of them.

Game in what? Well, 3NT would be a good proposition with (2) or (3) and by no means impossible on (1). West's One Heart was in a sense forced, and he may well have only a four-card suit. East could hold four hearts but not enough general strength to raise.

Thus, a jump to 3NT comes well into the picture. The danger is a singleton heart opposite. Partner can hold something like:

(4) ♠ Q x x x   ♡ x   ◇ A x x x   ♣ K x x x

I can avoid landing in 3NT opposite that hand by forcing with Two Hearts. That will extract a bid of 2NT (or Three Hearts) from him on hand (3), and on hand (4) we should find our way to Five Clubs. However, Two Hearts will not work out well when partner has no guard in hearts, for then we shall miss 3NT unless I bid it myself on the next round. If I intend to do that I might as well bid 3NT at once, with the psychological advantage that the defence will sometimes be discouraged from leading hearts.

It is this last consideration that inclines me to 3NT rather than 2NT. Partner will generally raise 2NT to Three, but the impression of a heart stop in my hand will be stronger when I bid 3NT myself.

Three and Four Clubs

Three Clubs, though better than a pass, would sound too defensive. With nothing in reserve after his redouble, North would often pass. The disadvantage of Four Clubs is that it goes beyond the likely game in 3NT.

Summing Up

Two Hearts would not be in any sense a mistake at this point. In a match it would be the right call, though South would have to take a further decision on the next round should partner sign off in Three Clubs. At rubber bridge 3NT strikes me as a good gamble and I mark the alternatives:

$$
\begin{array}{lr}
\text{3NT} & 10 \\
\text{Two Hearts} & 7 \\
\text{2NT} & 7 \\
\text{Three Clubs} & 4 \\
\text{Four Clubs} & 4 \\
\text{Pass} & 1 \\
\end{array}
$$

Reflections on the Bidding

When this situation occurred at the table South bid a watery Three Clubs. "Offensive-defensive" action is what he called it. But who wants to be defensive in this sequence? The clubs appear to be solid and partner has redoubled, so game in 3NT should be lay-down unless the opponents can run five heart tricks.

Why was it suggested that in a match South should make the safer call of Two Hearts? Because in a match the first objective should be to avoid action that may lead to an adverse swing. At rubber bridge, and also in a pairs tournament, a player must seize chances as they arise.

30. Not So Clever

My partner at rubber bridge is a competent and experienced player, familiar with modern styles of bidding. With both sides vulnerable I deal and pick up:

♠ Q 10 8 6 4   ♡ K Q 5   ◇ 10   ♣ A J 7 4

A slight problem about opening One Spade is that I have no good rebid over a response of Two Diamonds. I would have to choose between repeating the unrepeatable spades and bidding the non-existent hearts.

So ne players would seek a solution by opening One Club. That gets one past the first round, but other problems follow. It is difficult, without rebidding the suit at a dangerous level, to get it across that the spades are a five-card suit.

Since the main reason for opening is the possibility of game in spades, it would really be foolish to suppress the suit. So I open with **One Spade,** hoping to hear something other than Two Diamonds from partner. West, on my left, overcalls with **Two Hearts,** partner bids **Three Diamonds,** and East passes. That's worse still! I have to find a call after this sequence:

South	West	North	East
1♠	2♡	3◇	Pass
?			

The Alternatives

If I treat this bid of Three Diamonds as forcing, I must bid 3NT or Three Spades. No need to consider Four Clubs, which would be wildly unsound on this minimum hand. As I reserve the right to pass, the alternatives are:

3NT
Three Spades
Pass

The Choice

Assuming that I have to bid something (though I am going to question this later), which is better as between Three Spades and 3NT?

Three Spades will be bad when partner has no steam left and has to pass on a singleton or doubleton spade, perhaps holding a good six-card suit of diamonds. It may also be bad when, with a fair hand, he stretches to raise the spades on A x or K x.

It is easy to see that 3NT may come to ruin even when partner has fair values such as A K x x x x in diamonds and one of the black Kings. West will lead a heart, probably from a six-card suit headed by the Ace, and as soon as East gains the lead the defence will run five tricks in hearts.

3NT, if we make it, will at least win the rubber and there is something to be said for the theory that if you have to take a risk you should take one that is worthwhile. Still, we are vulnerable, and 3NT is much more likely to be doubled than Three Spades or even (if we get there) Four Spades. At rubber bridge it isn't clever to walk into a possible 1100 penalty.

Can I Pass Three Diamonds?

In theory, the change of suit is forcing at the Three level, just as it would be at the Two level. However, my partner is a sensible player and, if he had a game hand, I think he would look for a clearer call that wouldn't put me on the spot. Let's consider some possible holdings:

(1) ♠ K J x ♡ x x ◇ A Q J x x ♣ Q x x

Here he would give me Three Spades, not bid a pointless Three Diamonds. (There is actually a strong inference, for North, that I hold five spades. A player with only four spades, unless his second suit is hearts, will generally open a minor suit, especially on a moderate hand.)

Suppose next that North had solid diamonds and wanted me to bid 3NT if I could control the hearts:

(2) ♠ x x ♡ x x ◇ A K Q J x x ♣ K x x

Now, after One Spade—Two Hearts by West, the modern style

enjoins not Three Diamonds but Three Hearts. We play that as a general-purpose force, in this instance obviously asking for 3NT.

Could Three Diamonds Be a Disaster?

Unlikely, because the diamonds should be fairly strong. With a diamond suit such as A x x x x partner would usually be able to find a better bid. On balance of probabilities I think it much more likely that he has a fair hand with good diamonds, something like:

(3) ♠ x   ♡ x x   ◇ A Q 9 x x x   ♣ K 10 x x

If it's that sort of hand, then obviously neither Three Spades nor 3NT by me would be a success. I am going to pass before worse befalls, and I mark the alternatives:

Pass.........................10
Three Spades................. 6
3NT 4

Reflections on the Bidding

The suggestion that North should bid Three Hearts on hand (2) above will seem unusual to some readers, but the advantage of using the bid of the enemy suit in that sense is obvious. When that understanding exists, the change of suit in a sequence like this should not, in my opinion, be treated as unconditionally forcing.

Also worth noting is South's reason for judging Three Spades more prudent than 3NT. When you have to choose between two risky calls, prefer the one that is less likely to attract a double if the situation is as bad as you fear.

31. A Liability

With both sides vulnerable in a pairs event, the dealer on my right passes and in second position I hold:

♠ J 10   ♡ A K 9 5   ◇ J 9 7 6 2   ♣ 8 4

I pass and West opens **One Diamond**. My partner overcalls with **One Spade** and East passes. I have to find a call to reflect my modest values after the sequence:

South	West	North	East
—	—	—	Pass
Pass	1◇	1♠	Pass
?			

The Alternatives

The most aggressive action I can contemplate is Two Hearts, the least aggressive is a pass. The natural bids in between are 1NT or Two Spades. That seems to cover the field:

> Two Spades
> Two Hearts
> 1NT
> Pass

The Choice

This is probably a part-score hand, but if anyone can make game it is more likely to be our side than theirs. Four Spades, 3NT and even Four Hearts are all within reach if partner's overcall is close to a maximum. On those grounds alone we can rule out a pass.

Whose Hand Is It?

This question asks, "If both sides do the best they can, who will end up with a plus score?" Supposing here that our maximum is eight tricks in spades, is it likely that they can outbid us, presumably in clubs?

There is no certainty about this, but we hold the majors and East did not bid on the first round. It is more likely to be our hand than theirs, but they could, of course, have a good fit in clubs.

The reason for considering a theoretical point of this sort is to judge whether a tactical rather than a descriptive bid is called for. If I thought that we were likely to be outbid on the hand I might incline toward a bid such as Two Spades. This would raise the level of the auction and might prevent the opponents from getting together. I intend to make what I think is the accurate call, however, as I do not particularly fear competition.

Two Hearts an Exaggeration

There are obvious objections to Two Hearts. The suit is weak, hearts are not a likely spot for the two hands, and once I make this encouraging call I have shot my bolt and cannot do any more bidding. The best that can be said for Two Hearts is that it tells partner where my high cards are.

1NT or Two Spades?

The choice surely lies between these two and I can find many more arguments for 1NT than for Two Spades. Most important of these is that the diamonds should pull plenty of weight at no trump but their length may be a liability in spades. If we play in Three or Four Spades I can foresee a diamond lead and ruff, West put in with a club, another diamond lead, and so on.

It is slightly unorthodox to bid 1NT with a small doubleton in a side suit, but at this level it won't matter greatly if the opponents run the first five tricks in clubs. There will be some rubbish to be put in the basket while this goes on.

One might say too that it would be unorthodox to support the spades on a doubleton. In a general way I am not nervous about supporting an overcall on J 10, but there seems no tactical reason to do so here. As we noted, the hand may play badly in spades, and this is not the moment to raise on minimum trumps.

Finally, when there is a choice of calls I think it is a sound principle to choose the one that leaves the bidder with something in reserve. Thus, if I bid 1NT now I have some breath left and can bid Two Spades over Two Clubs. Similarly, if partner jumps to Three Spades over 1NT I can give him Four without stretching. Players who follow the principle of keeping a bit in reserve seldom have to let their partners "hang" one trick short of game.

I have shown where my preference lies and I mark the alternatives:

$$
\begin{array}{ll}
\text{1NT} & \dots\dots\dots\dots\dots\dots\dots 10 \\
\text{Two Spades} & \dots\dots\dots\dots\dots\dots 6 \\
\text{Two Hearts} & \dots\dots\dots\dots\dots\dots 3 \\
\text{Pass} & \dots\dots\dots\dots\dots\dots\dots 3 \\
\end{array}
$$

Reflections on the Bidding

This is one of those problems where the average player is more likely to agree with my answer of 1NT than the more advanced player, who in these competitive positions tends to prefer the more obstructive bid of Two Spades.

Nevertheless, I am inclined to say that the expert who votes for Two Spades is guilty of lazy thinking. Remember the main points I have stressed here. There is no need to be obstructive, the diamonds will help in no trump but not in spades, and the hand may in fact play badly in spades.

32. Positional Play

Playing in a pairs event against opponents who normally play a sound game, I hold in second position:

♠ Q 8 3   ♡ 7 4   ◇ K Q 9 2   ♣ A 10 7 3

Neither side is vulnerable and East, on my right, opens **One Spade.** I pass and West responds **1NT.** This is **doubled** by my partner and East bids **Two Hearts.** It is not easy to express my values after the sequence:

South	West	North	East
—	—	—	1♠
Pass	1NT	Double	2♡
?			

The Alternatives

The first call that comes to mind is Three Hearts which, as we play it nowadays, would be a force to game but would not promise any strength in hearts. If partner could be relied on to read it in the same sense, Two Spades would be at least as good. Three Clubs or Three Diamonds would be safe. Finally, I might rely on partner to have some strength in hearts and bid either 2NT or 3NT myself. On that basis the alternatives are:

    3NT
    2NT
    Three Hearts
    Three Diamonds
    Three Clubs
    Two Spades

I haven't included Four Clubs or Four Diamonds because if I had my eyes on game in a minor suit the first step would be a force of Three Hearts.

My hand is surprisingly strong in view of all the bidding. Allowing West a minimum of 6 points for his 1NT, and East a shapely 10 points, there is just room for partner to hold 13. As he doubled 1NT after only spades had been bid against him, he must have been prepared for a heart response. I imagine he holds something of this sort:

(1) ♠ x   ♡ A J x x   ◇ A x x x   ♣ K J x x

(2) ♠ x x   ♡ A x x   ◇ A 10 x x   ♣ K Q x x

(3) ♠ x   ♡ K Q 10   ◇ A x x x   ♣ K J x x x

The double would be risky on any of these hands, but in a pairs event such aggression is normal. At any rate, I do not suspect our present opponents of psychic bidding.

One point that is plain from these examples is that the chances of game are better in no trump than in a suit. At least one of the minor suits is likely to break 4-1.

Having reached that conclusion we should be able to strike out some of the alternatives. Let's examine them in turn.

Three Clubs or Three Diamonds

Either minor should be safe, but we can probably make a better score at no trump.

Two Spades

Being short in spades himself, partner might take this to be a genuine suit. From his point of view I might be sitting over the spade bidder with a holding such as Q J 9 8 x x. I am not going to take that risk.

Three Hearts

Can I be sure that he would read this as a request to bid 3NT? He might think that if I held spades I would bid no trump myself, relying on him to control the hearts. Apart from this, I am not at all sure that a no trump contract would play well from his side. If East opened a spade through my Q x x and West held something like K 10 x, we would lose five or six tricks at once. If West had K 10 alone, and East had Ace of hearts as an entry, again they could run the tricks.

2NT and 3NT

It is unlikely that partner will be able to raise 2NT to Three and, at aggregate scoring, I would take a chance on 3NT. In a pairs event, however, to make 2NT with an overtrick should be a good enough result. Most pairs will be scoring 110 or so in a minor suit. If partner takes out 2NT into Three Clubs or Three Diamonds, I shall have to think again. For the moment, 2NT seems the best balanced call and I mark the alternatives:

2NT	10
3NT	8
Three Hearts	5
Three Diamonds	5
Three Clubs	5
Two Spades	1

Reflections on the Bidding

This was a difficult but instructive problem, since it was possible to form a very close estimate of partner's strength and distribution. Also worth noting was the reflection that 2NT in a pairs tournament would result in a better-than-average score even if nine tricks could be made.

In pointing out the danger of laying the spade holding on the table, I had the benefit of hindsight. When the situation occurred in actual play, South did bid Three Hearts and North, who held hand (2) above, read his partner's intentions well and bid 3NT. Unfortunately, a spade *was* led, West held three to an honor, and the first five tricks went to the defence.

33. Something in Hand

In a match-pointed pairs event, both sides are vulnerable and in third position I hold:

♠ 7 5 3 2   ♡ 8 6 4 2   ◇ A K 3   ♣ K J

My partner deals and opens **One Club.** East overcalls with **One Spade** and even at this low level I have a decided problem after the sequence:

South	West	North	East
—	—	1♣	1♠
?			

The Alternatives

This is a problem that players would solve in various ways according to bidding style. Some would pass, relying on partner to reopen if necessary. Some would double, expecting partner to pass only if the double suited him. Some would make modest bids such as 1NT or Two Clubs. Two Diamonds would be rather more aggressive. Some players would seek a solution by bidding the opponent's suit. If we include all these calls, the alternatives are:

Two Spades
Two Diamonds
Two Clubs
1NT
Double
Pass

There is one style of bidding that deals satisfactorily with this type of situation. That is the "negative" or "sputnik" double of the Roth-Stone system, which conveys the message: "I have a few good cards but my hand is not well suited for any positive bid."

It would be agreeable to be playing the convention on this hand, but we shall have to manage without it. Where it is apparent that no call is ideal, the only approach is to examine the virtues and defects of the alternatives.

Pass

This can be right only for players who set a high value on free bids and rely on their partners to "balance," as it is called. If West passed they would expect North, with little more than a minimum opening, to keep the bidding alive. In my opinion that is a difficult way to play the game, but this is not a theoretical discussion.

In the absence of a highly developed balancing technique, the disadvantage of passing is that too often the opponents will obtain the contract in One Spade when we have the majority of the cards.

Double

This is another call that can be considered only on the basis that a double at the level of One is co-operative and should be left in only by a partner who likes it well. That is a playable method, but not general, so there is no point in discussing its merits on this hand. If a double would have the normal sense of a penalty double, it might sometimes register 200, but it could also be disastrous.

1NT

This call expresses the values well enough but is open to the powerful objection that a no trump contract will be played from the wrong side if partner has a spade guard such as K x. Apart from that, of course, you may find yourself in 1NT or more with no guard at all. That will not matter so much at the One level.

Two Clubs

The trump support is below standard, but there is compensation in that the high card strength is better than normal for this raise. It is true that partner may have opened a short suit, but it should still be possible to run six or seven tricks in high cards.

The long-term advantage of Two Clubs is that, having made what in a sense is an underbid on an A K and a K J, you can co-operate in any further venture by partner. If he bids Two Hearts or 2NT, for example, you can raise freely. When we look at the next two bids we shall find a difference in that respect.

Two Diamonds

This change of suit is forcing and the difficulty will be to judge the right action on the next round. If partner bids Three Clubs, you can pass; if he bids Three Diamonds, you must try to make it. Two Hearts you must raise, though you will be on somewhat dangerous ground by this time. The most awkward rebid is the most likely one, 2NT. In a sense your 11 points will justify a raise to Three, but if partner is minimum—and remember, he had to call something—you may be out of your depth.

Two Spades

This bid is open to the same objection to a much worse degree. Assuming you play the call simply as a general-purpose force to game, what are you going to do on the next round? Suppose, for example, that partner bids Three Clubs. Are you going to double-cross him by passing? Or will you press on till you reach game somewhere?

Summing Up

In this unpleasant position I feel that Two Clubs is the call least likely to do immediate damage as well as the easiest to follow up. 1NT and Two Diamonds have some merits but also specific disadvantages. I mark the alternatives:

Reflections on the Bidding

This problem brings out a point we noted in problem 31. When confronted with a choice of calls of which none is satisfactory, he disposed toward the one that is easiest to follow up. So, of the two most sensible bids, prefer Two Clubs to Two Diamonds. Do not deliberately start something you may not have the strength to finish.

34. Untimely Intervention

Playing in a team-of-four match with I.M.P. scoring, I hold as dealer:

♠ A J 7 5 3 ♡ A K J ♢ 6 3 2 ♣ A 7

Our side is vulnerable and I open **One Spade.** Partner responds **Two Clubs** and East intervenes with **Three Diamonds.** It is not going to be easy to find an accurate bid after the sequence:

South	West	North	East
1♠	Pass	2♣	3♢
?			

The Alternatives

One way to ensure progress is to bid the enemy suit. Such rebids as Three Spades, Three Hearts, and Four Clubs must come into consideration. A pass would be well chosen if partner could be relied on to bid again. A double would bring in points more often than not. The alternatives are certainly numerous:

> Four Diamonds
> Four Clubs
> Three Spades
> Three Hearts
> Double
> Pass

The Choice

This pre-empt by the non-vulnerable opponent is probably based on seven top diamonds, but it may also be just a nuisance bid on K Q J 10 x x x and some distributional quirk. If so, it has achieved its object. Opposite partner's response at the level of Two I have the values to expect a game, but now I lack space in which to explore the right denomination.

Had East intervened with Two Diamonds I would have had two reasonable bids open to me: Three Diamonds, asking partner to bid 3NT or describe his hand in some other way, and Two Hearts. This last bid would be irregular, but I would have some room in which to escape from a game contract with inadequate trumps. We might begin by studying the effect of these bids at the higher level to which we have been pushed.

Four Diamonds

A cue-bid of the opponent's suit, with 3NT already behind us, would be taken as confirming clubs and promising at least second-round control of diamonds. We might land on our feet in Five Clubs but all future bidding would be guesswork.

Three Hearts

This might pass off all right. There would be no problem if partner bid Three Spades or Four Clubs. Less welcome would be a raise to Four Hearts. I would either have to try to make it, with the prospect of dummy's four trumps being forced immediately, or transfer to Five Clubs.

Perhaps the worst that could happen over Three Hearts is that partner, having stretched already to bid Two Clubs, would pass, holding three small trumps. A new suit at the Three level is normally forcing, but North would have to allow here for the possibility that I had been pushed high by the intervention. In his position I wouldn't treat Three Hearts as forcing.

Pass

That cannot be right, for it is quite likely that partner will be unable to continue. He will place East with some of the Aces I hold.

Double

This would have to be considered at rubber bridge, where to accept a probable 300 in place of a problematical game is never wrong. At I.M.P. scoring, to take 300 in place of a vulnerable game, not to mention a slam, costs several points and the chance of game here is too good to pass up.

Three Spades

Such overstatement of the spade strength could be disastrous, as this suit may be strongly held by West. It cannot be right to play in spades until partner has volunteered support.

Four Clubs

The trump support is well below normal for what in effect is a double raise, but that may be only a technical objection. Partner is likely to have one of two types of hand, of which the first will contain a long club suit, such as:

$$(1) \spadesuit Q x \quad \heartsuit x x x \quad \diamondsuit x x \quad \clubsuit K Q J x x x$$

Some players are forbidden by their system to respond at the level of Two on such a hand, but my present partner is happily not of those. Having stretched already he would pass Four Clubs (and also Three Hearts, with less success!).

With a better hand of this type, North will advance to Five Clubs or, if stronger still, make a cue-bid in diamonds.

The other type of hand is:

$$(2) \spadesuit K 10 x \quad \heartsuit Q x x x \quad \diamondsuit x x \quad \clubsuit K Q x x$$

When the clubs are moderate, as in this example, he will have secondary support for spades.

If one is going to make an irregular call, the objections to Four Clubs are less than those to Three Hearts, and I mark the alternatives:

Four Clubs	10
Three Hearts	8
Double	5
Four Diamonds	5
Pass	2
Three Spades	1

Reflections on the Bidding

When this situation arose at the table, North had a freakish 1-5-0-7 hand, with Q 10 x x x of hearts and K Q J 10 x x of clubs. A grand slam could have been made in either suit and almost any bid would have led to Six.

South's problem over Three Diamonds was difficult and at the time I thought his actual choice, Three Hearts, was the best. Closer study inclined me to Four Clubs, for the reasons given above. The situation is analogous to that when partner has made a defensive overcall and it becomes apparent from the bidding that all he can have is a strong suit. Having reached that conclusion one sometimes raises on a low doubleton and some tricks outside. On the present occasion the odds were that partner held good clubs—there wasn't room for anything else. That being so, the raise in clubs came clearly into the picture.

35. The Defence Is Tricky

In a team event, with I.M.P. scoring, our side is vulnerable and in fourth position I hold:

♠ Q J 9 7 4   ♡ Q J 6 3   ◇ J 7 3   ♣ 5

West, on my left, opens **1NT.** They are playing a weak 1NT when not vulnerable, about 12 to 14 points. My partner **doubles** and East passes. I have a difficult call after this short sequence:

South	West	North	East
—	1NT	Double	Pass
?			

The Alternatives

I can pass the double and probably collect a small penalty, or I can try for a vulnerable game. There are two aggressive bids—Three Spades or 2NT, which would be conventional and forcing. Two Spades would be a safe compromise. The alternatives are:

Three Spades
Two Spades
2NT
Pass

The Choice

Although the opponents are playing a weak no trump, my partner is in an exposed position and I expect him to hold upward of 15 points. We surely have the balance of the cards and, barring accidents, should be able to defeat 1NT. At rubber bridge it wouldn't be wrong to accept a penalty of 300, but at duplicate that would be a poor exchange for a vulnerable game. Also, it may be difficult to play the right defence against 1NT doubled. Partner will have to lead from strength, he won't know about my spade suit, and if we lose an early tempo declarer may make tricks in clubs. Actually, I never like passing 1NT doubled at this score unless my hand is weak and balanced.

Chances of Game

After an opponent has opened 1NT, it is easier to play the hand than to defend. The position of the cards is marked, the strong defender has to make the leads, and 3NT can often be made on two or three points less than the standard 24 to 25. Similarly, if partner has support for spades, game in that suit should not present any problem.

Three Spades or 2NT?

There are two ways of approaching game. 2NT in this position is a conventional force, for with a moderate balanced hand I would pass the double. Partner will bid his best suit and then I can show my spades, leaving him to choose the final contract.

The alternative is a direct jump to Three Spades. Since 2NT is available as a forcing take-out, the jump in a suit should be non-forcing, in my opinion. The only objection to it is that partner might take me for a more distributional hand, such as:

$$\spadesuit \text{Q } 10 \text{ x x x x} \quad \heartsuit \text{x} \quad \diamondsuit \text{K x x x} \quad \clubsuit \text{x x}$$

Three Spades would be right on that sort of hand, where I would want to be in game unless partner had a singleton spade. If I make that bid on the present hand we may play in Three or Four Spades when 3NT would be better.

Two Spades Too Conservative

A simple take-out into Two Spades would guarantee a five-card suit, it is true, as with only four-card suits I would choose the lowest so as to give partner more room. However, Two Spades would not promise anything in high cards and partner would seldom be able to continue. If I am not going to play for the vulnerable game I may as well pass and hope for 300 or more.

Since I am optimistic about the chances of game, I mark the alternatives:

2NT 10
Three Spades 8
Pass 5
Two Spades 4

Reflections on the Bidding

Responding to a double of 1NT is often tricky because partner cannot be relied on to have support for any particular suit. The points that have emerged from this discussion are:

When playing against a 12-14 no trump, it is too dangerous in North's position to intervene on a hand of similar strength. Unless he holds a good suit, his minimum for a double should be about 15 points.

In South's position at this score it seldom pays on an unbalanced hand to pass the double for penalties. The defence is apt to go astray and sometimes declarer has a concealed suit and makes 1NT doubled with much less than half the total honor strength.

On responding hands where there is a choice of contracts, 2NT is a valuable first move. It asks partner to bid his best suit and makes it possible to explore in more than one direction.

36. Deterrent Factor

At rubber bridge the vulnerable opponent on my right deals and passes. My hand is

♠ Q 8 4   ♡ A K 8   ◇ Q J 10   ♣ K Q 10 4

As I am too strong for 1NT not vulnerable in the Acol system, I open **One Club.** West overcalls with One Diamond and partner bids **One Spade.** East passes and I have a rebid problem after this sequence:

South	West	North	East
—	—	—	Pass
1♣	1◇	1♠	Pass
?			

The Alternatives

In terms of general value the hand is worth 2NT. Other bids of about the same strength are Three Spades or a reverse of Two Hearts. If I regard West's overcall of One Diamond as a deterrent factor, I can hold back with 1NT or Two Spades. Two Diamonds, as a general force asking partner to declare himself further, is another possibility. If we include that, the alternatives are:

Three Spades
Two Spades
2NT
1NT
Two Hearts
Two Diamonds

The Choice

The normal rebid in our system on a balanced 17 points is 2NT, but after West's overcall that seems unattractive. West would not have come in vulnerable after his partner had passed unless he had a good suit and some tricks. After a diamond lead, unless my partner can contribute a second stop, we shall have to run nine tricks straight off. There are many hands on which partner would bid 3NT where we

125

would go down two, losing five diamonds and an Ace. And if partner had to pass 2NT, I would not expect to make it.

A Bid of the Enemy Suit

Two Diamonds, using a bid of the enemy suit as a general force, would ask partner to describe his hand further. It would be agreeable if partner were able to show a diamond stop by bidding 2NT, but unless that happened the manoeuvre would take us no further. For example, if partner were now to bid Three Clubs or Two Spades I would have no idea whether to continue. Theoretically, I ought not to pass short of game.

The Other Strong Calls

What of Two Hearts? Having shown a good hand by the reverse, I would be free to pass Two Spades, but either Three Hearts or Three Clubs would be embarrassing.

A jump to Three Spades would be an overbid by any standards—the more so with the prospect of a diamond lead and continuation.

Two Spades or 1NT?

I am going to choose one of the more conservative bids but I haven't made up my mind yet as between Two Spades and 1NT. The distribution suggests no trump, but in view of the diamond overcall, game in spades is perhaps more likely. I am thinking of this sort of responding hand:

$$\spadesuit K J 10 x x \quad \heartsuit J x x \quad \diamondsuit x x \quad \clubsuit A x x$$

With such a dummy there would be no play for 3NT but we would have a good chance for Four Spades.

Two Spades is slightly more encouraging than 1NT, and it does not exclude our playing in no trump. If over Two Spades partner can muster Three Spades or Three Clubs, I can bid 3NT. He will leave that if he has three small diamonds or, unexpectedly, a diamond honor. As a matter of fact, when one constructs possible holdings for partner it becomes evident that Two Spades is scarcely an underbid. Finally, if partner is weak, 1NT can fail more easily than Two Spades for we could quickly lose five diamonds and two Aces. I mark the alternatives:

Reflections on the Bidding

The problem illustrates that when there is a long suit against you the normal standard of 25 points for 3NT has no meaning. What you want, in addition to a guard, is a long suit of your own and *Aces*. Suppose that in the present example the opposite hand had been:

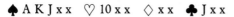 A K J x x   ♡ 10 x x   ◇ x x   ♣ J x x

Now the spades are good for five tricks, but to make 3NT after a diamond lead you want Ace of clubs instead of the combined K Q J.

37. Degrees of Apprehension

In a team-of-four match I am last to speak and hold:

♠ 9 5 3 2   ♡ A J 3   ◇ A Q 6   ♣ 8 3 2

With neither side vulnerable West, on my left, opens **One Spade**. My partner **doubles** and East passes. The situation is familiar but never easy to resolve satisfactorily:

South	West	North	East
—	1♠	Double	Pass
?			

The Alternatives

Players who treat 1NT as a constructive reply to a double may be content with that here. A jump to 2NT, despite the absence of a spade guard, would better reflect the values. A bid of the opponent's suit, Two Spades, would be forcing for the present. If none of these seems satisfactory, one can bid Two Diamonds and hope that something will develop. That seems to cover both likely and unlikely alternatives:

2NT
1NT
Two Spades
Two Diamonds

The Choice

There is a theory that 1NT in response to a double should promise fair values and not always a guard in the enemy suit. That is a useful understanding to have on some occasions, and I agree that 1NT in response to the double of a minor should be better than a minimum. Over a major suit, such an arrangement is less satisfactory. It means that with K J 10 x in the enemy suit and 4-3-3-3 distribution one is debarred from making the only sensible call. Thus, on a point of theory

I do not accept that 1NT should be regarded as constructive in the present sequence. Even if it were, two Aces, a Queen and a Jack would be over the maximum.

The other non-constructive bid, Two Diamonds, would generally result in a plus score, but that's about all one can say. Partner would seldom be able to advance and game would often be missed.

Two Spades Only Postpones the Decision

A frequent answer in these positions where one thinks there should be a game somewhere is to bid the enemy suit. Here Two Spades seems to me to postpone the decision without resolving it. Unless partner can bid 2NT, which is not likely, you are not much further on whatever he calls. Three Hearts you will raise to Four, but 3NT might be a better contract. Three Diamonds or Three Clubs will leave you in the air, uncertain whether to pass, raise the suit, or take a chance on 3NT, trusting him to realize that you are not altogether happy about your stop in spades.

2NT a Reasonable Hazard

2NT is the only bid that presents a picture of the general values, but it is, of course, open to the objection that the spades are not well held. Partner will not often raise to Three, however, without some bolster in the suit. Let us look at one or two possible hands:

$$(1) \spadesuit x \quad \heartsuit K x x x \quad \diamondsuit K x x \quad \clubsuit A Q x x x$$

With a moderate 5-4-3-1 hand he will usually take out into the long suit. If he passes 2NT you may make it.

$$(2) \spadesuit Q x \quad \heartsuit K Q x x \quad \diamondsuit K 10 x x \quad \clubsuit A J x$$

Now he will raise to 3NT and there is a fair chance that the spades will be blocked—if East holds J x or 10 x, for example.

Even when partner has as little as 10 x in spades, it by no means follows that they will run a long suit against you. Sometimes the suit will divide 4-3; at other times it will be blocked. For example, West, holding A K J x x, may start with the King and then be unable to run the tricks.

I'm not really nervous about bidding 2NT. If one speaks of nerves, I should await the dummy with much greater apprehension if I had made the massive underbid of 1NT or Two Diamonds. I mark the alternatives:

$$2NT \dotfill 10$$
$$\text{Two Spades} \dotfill 6$$
$$\text{Two Diamonds} \dotfill 4$$
$$1NT \dotfill 4$$

Reflections on the Bidding

Most players would make this bid of 2NT at rubber bridge, I am sure, and if it is a good proposition there it should also be at duplicate. It is quite true that in match play it is wise to avoid irregular action that may lead to an adverse game swing, but there is no assurance here that the bidding at the other table will follow the same course. Perhaps West will make a different opening, or not open at all, or perhaps North will make a different overcall. At any rate, it is quite likely, in view of the combined values held by North-South, that they will sail into game somewhere.

38. Avoiding Ambiguity

In a team event both sides are vulnerable and in fourth position I hold:

♠ 7 6 2   ♡ A 7   ◇ A 9 5 4 2   ♣ A 6 3

After two passes East, on my right, opens **One Diamond.** I pass, and West responds **Two Clubs.** Partner now enters with a **double.** East passes and I have to reassess my hand after the sequence:

South	West	North	East
—	Pass	Pass	1◇
Pass	2♣	Double	Pass
?			

The Alternatives

North's double, following an original pass, indicates a desire to play in one of the unbid suits. If game seems unlikely, I can bid Two Spades or let the double stand. If I decide to try for game I can jump in spades or make a more scientific approach with Two Diamonds or Three Clubs. To bid no trump at any level would surely be misguided, so the alternatives are:

Three Spades
Two Spades
Three Clubs
Two Diamonds
Pass

The Choice

Partner has come in vulnerable at the Two level and I feel that he must either be close to an opening bid, with at least nine cards in the majors, or be strong distributionally. Let's begin by looking at a few hands and seeing whether they fit in with his bidding so far.

(1) ♠ K J x x x   ♡ K x x x x   ◇ x   ♣ x x

Not strong enough to risk entry at this point.

(2) ♠ K Q J x ♡ K Q 10 x x ◇ x ♣ x x x

If his distribution is 5-4 he will not be weaker than this. The following hands are nearer to what I would expect:

(3) ♠ K J 10 x x ♡ K Q 9 x x ◇ x x ♣ x

(4) ♠ A J x x x ♡ Q J x x x x ◇ x ♣ x

(5) ♠ A x x x x x ♡ K J x x x ◇ x ♣ x

Putting these hands opposite mine, two things become clear: It would be a mistake to pass the double, which would be a success only opposite hand (2), and there are definite chances of game. Thus, we can eliminate a pass and reject Two Spades as inadequate.

Two Diamonds Would Be Ambiguous

Of the stronger calls, Two Diamonds would keep the bidding at a low level but would be open to misunderstanding. It might look to partner as though I could not assist in the majors but had a long string of diamonds and was willing to play in that suit. His own shortage in diamonds would point to that conclusion. He might take out into a six-card suit of his own but he would not be wrong to pass on (2) or (3) above.

Three Clubs More Flexible Than Three Spades

A jump to Three Spades would not be far wrong on values but would sometimes land us in the wrong suit. On hand (4), for example, Four Hearts would play better than Four Spades.

A force of Three Clubs enables us to bid the hand with greater accuracy. If partner has longer spades than hearts, he will bid Three Spades and I will go to game. When he has longer hearts than spades he will bid Three Hearts and I will transfer to Three Spades. He will know that I am able to stand Four Hearts as well. When he has equal length in the two suits, as on hand (3) above, his correct bid technically will be Three Diamonds and then again I will bid Three Spades.

This seems to deal satisfactorily with all possibilities and I mark the alternatives:

> Three Clubs..................10
> Three Spades................. 7
> Two Spads.................. 4
> Two Diamonds 2
> Pass........................ 1

Reflections on the Bidding

It was possible to form a fairly close picture of partner's hand after he had passed originally and then stepped in vulnerable at the range of Two when the opponents were still unlimited. Game was seen to be a distinct possibility and Three Clubs was the best call because it gave the maximum chance of finishing in the longer suit. In situations where trump control is likely to be a factor, it is important to realize that a trump suit divided 6-2 is preferable to one divided 5-3, and that 5-2 is better than 4-3.

39. Maintaining Course

In a pairs event neither side is vulnerable and I hold in third position:

♠ 10 5   ♡ Q 10 7 6 3   ◇ K J 10   ♣ 8 7 5

My partner deals and opens **2NT**—about 20-22 points in our system. East overcalls with **Three Spades,** presenting me with a small problem:

South	West	North	East
—	—	2NT	3♠
?			

The Alternatives

I might disregard East's overcall and bid 3NT. I could seek to chasten him with a double. Four Hearts is a possibility and if none of those actions appeared suitable I could pass. The alternatives are:

Four Hearts
3NT
Double
Pass

The Choice

One call we can eliminate quickly is a pass. Unless partner has bid an unorthodox 2NT we should be able to beat Three Spades by a trick or two. If East has such a freak that he can make nine tricks in spades, that will be a bad result for us whether the contract is doubled or not.

We might collect 300 by doubling Three Spades, but 500 seems unlikely. East probably has seven or eight tricks in his own hand. If game is on we cannot afford, in a pairs tournament, to accept a moderate penalty.

What Are the Chances of Game?

If East had passed I would have raised to 3NT with fair expectation of making it. I'm not sure that East's Three Spades makes much difference to our prospects. If East had a suit such as K Q J 9 x x with an Ace

134

outside, he would have been more inclined to pass 2NT, with a good chance of beating it. It is more likely that he has a long suit with no entry, or a broken suit.

Four Hearts or 3NT?

Oddly enough, the overcall is a greater threat to Four Hearts than to 3NT. The lead would be through partner's spade holding and the hearts might be badly divided. Since I wasn't going to try for game in hearts if East had passed, I certainly won't do so now. I mark the alternatives:

> 3NT 10
> Double 5
> Four Hearts................. 3
> Pass........................ 2

Reflections on the Bidding

This was not a difficult bid to find, but the point made about East's overcall is worth remembering. It applies equally at the range of Two. When partner opens 1NT and the defender overcalls with Two of a suit, that suit is generally broken. When the partner of the no trump bidder has a clear raise to game, barring the intervention, he should not as a rule be deflected by lack of a guard in the enemy suit.

40. Time to Listen

In a pairs event our side is vulnerable and I hold as dealer:

♠ J 5 4   ♡ A   ◇ 8 7 6   ♣ A K Q 8 3 2

I open **One Club,** West passes, and my partner responds **One Spade.** This is **doubled** by East. I have to search for the best tactical rebid after the sequence:

South	West	North	East
1♣	Pass	1♠	Double
?			

The Alternatives

A simple rebid of Two Clubs or a raise to Two Spades would sufficiently express the high-card values, but a jump to Three Clubs is a possibility, and so is a defensive Three Spades, if one assumes that partner will have a fair suit in this sequence. I could seek to inhibit the enemy by redoubling. Some players might fancy a semi-psychic rebid of 1NT or even 2NT, but at the present vulnerability that seems a doubtful move. If we leave that out, the alternatives are:

Three Spades
Two Spades
Three Clubs
Two Clubs
Redouble

The Choice

When the rebid is affected by an element of competition, one can begin by studying what the hand is worth and then consider the tactical situation.

136

Had there been no intervention I would have judged the hand worth Three Clubs in terms of playing tricks. However, I would not bid more than Two Clubs because, with so many high cards missing, the bidding is likely to continue, and Three Clubs might excite partner too much. I want an opportunity to show my spade support, so it would be awkward if Three Clubs were to produce 3NT from partner.

In support of spades I certainly don't consider the hand worth more than a single raise. If hearts are played early, partner will need good spades in order to draw trumps and run the clubs. Equally, the pattern of the hand is not suitable for a ruffing game. There may be hearts to ruff, but not enough entries to the North hand.

Redouble

Turning to the competitive angle, I don't see much advantage in redoubling. The hand has two features I wish to show—good clubs and moderate support for spades—and a redouble would make no progress in either direction. Also, it would be unsound to redouble now and follow with Three Spades over an opposing Three Hearts or Three Diamonds.

Three Clubs

This has some pre-emptive value and expresses the general strength. The only disadvantage is that opponents will probably not be silenced, and I may be faced on the next round with a difficult decision whether or not to contest further with Three Spades.

Three Spades and Two Spades

The hand is worth so much more in clubs than spades that it seems bad timing to raise the spades now and probably be unable later to rebid the clubs. A jump to Three Spades is plausible only on the basis that a partner who responds One Spade to One Club on a moderate hand will necessarily have five spades—the modern style being to respond in a lower suit when possible. Even if one accepts that, and I do not, nine tricks in spades will still be hard to make when partner holds something like five spades to the Ace plus the King of hearts. East's double makes it seem likely that at least one of the black suits will divide badly.

Two Clubs

This bid gives up any pre-emptive notion, but has advantages in the way of accurate expression. Suppose that West bids Two of a red suit and this is followed by two passes. Then my rebid of Two Spades will be just right. If, instead, partner is able to make a free bid of Two Spades himself, that clears up all problems. If diamonds are bid by West and raised by East, then I will hazard Three Spades, taking partner to be short in diamonds and so to have some length in the black suits. A problem will arise only if West bids Two Hearts, partner passes, and East raises to Three. If that happens I shall probably pass, for they may well be on their way to Four and I have no intention of defending at that level.

The simple bid, Two Clubs, enables me to express my hand accurately and also to *listen* so that I can form an idea of how high to go. That seems to outweigh any advantage that can be gained by a mild pre-empt, and I mark the alternatives:

Two Clubs.................... 10
Three Clubs................. 8
Two Spades.................. 4
Redouble 4
Three Spades............... 1

Reflections on the Bidding

Defensive jumps are all very well in their place—which is when you know that your side is outgunned and the only question is how high you dare go to prevent opponents from exchanging information. When, as here, the issue of the hand is uncertain, it can be a mistake to abandon normal development. Three Clubs may silence partner as well as the opposition; he will not take it as an invitation to repeat his spades. Still more important, as was stressed above, is that the quiet bid gives you the best chance to gauge the general lie of the cards.

Many players, I think, would overestimate the South hand in support of spades. Compare the original hand with another that has the same high cards and distribution:

(1) ♠ J 5 4　♡ A　◇ 8 7 6　♣ A K Q 8 3 2

(2) ♠ J 5 4　♡ 6　◇ A 8 7　♣ A K Q 8 3 2

Hand (2) is much stronger. The entry for the clubs cannot be knocked out so readily; there is second round control of every suit; and if partner has one or two entries such as King of diamonds or Jack of clubs, he may be able to negotiate several ruffs in hearts. Yet for players who witlessly compute their values in terms of high-card and distributional points, the two hands are the same.

41. The Burning Deck

Both sides are vulnerable in a pairs event and in fourth position I hold:

♠ 7 5 4   ♡ A   ◇ 10 8 6 3   ♣ A K Q 10 4

West, on my left, opens **One Spade,** and this is followed by two passes. Some able practitioners of the match-point game would bid 1NT on my hand at this point, disregarding the shortage in hearts, not to mention the lack of a spade stop. I will say only that I could bear either one of these defects, but not the two together when I have a sound alternative in **Two Clubs.** West now bids **Two Diamonds,** my partner comes in with **Two Hearts,** and East passes. This is not altogether a happy development, the bidding having gone:

South	West	North	East
—	1♠	Pass	Pass
2♣	2◇	2♡	Pass
?			

The Alternatives

I can pass Two Hearts, rather hoping that West will continue, or I can go back to Three Clubs. 2NT might also be an improvement on the present contract. There is nothing else to consider, so the alternatives are:

Three Clubs
2NT
Pass

The Choice

At rubber bridge, or even at I.M.P., I might pass Two Hearts, satisfied that I could defend my action in the post-mortem. However, pairs events are won by points, not arguments, and I am going to consider carefully before leaving partner in Two Hearts.

The omens, it seems to me, are inauspicious. Partner did not overcall on the first round and while he *could* have a rock-ribbed suit such as K Q J x x x he could also, at match points, be contesting on a much weaker suit. At this point of the auction he would contest on any of these hands:

(1) ♠ A x x ♡ K Q 9 x x ◇ J x x ♣ J x

(2) ♠ Q 10 x x ♡ K J 10 x x ◇ K x ♣ x x

(3) ♠ A J x ♡ Q 10 8 x x x ◇ J x ♣ x x

East is *very* likely to have long hearts. He has not supported spades or diamonds, and an additional pointer is that if West had not been short of hearts—if he had held 5-3-4-1 distribution—he might have doubled on the second round in preference to bidding Two Diamonds.

Even if North has a good heart suit, such as Q J 10 x x x, the play can proceed awkwardly for him. East will be short in one if not both of his partner's suits, and an embarrassing sequence of plays is easy to foresee.

Will Three Clubs Be Better?

Possibly, but it is a range higher and again East may succeed in ruffing North's high cards in spades and diamonds.

How Will 2NT Fare?

Distinctly better when partner has the sort of hand shown in the examples above, and not necessarily worse on the occasions when West has five top winners in one of his suits. Against Two Hearts, if West can begin with four top cards in spades or diamonds, East will dispose of clubs and North will have a most unpleasant journey.

Summing Up

A final point for 2NT is that partner is free to return to Three Clubs or even to Three Hearts if his intermediates in that suit form a solid sequence. He should not overestimate the general strength of my hand, or my spade holding, because on the first round I made the simple protective bid of Two Clubs.

Three Clubs is less likely than Two Hearts to earn the kiss of death —minus 200 on a part-score hand. However, that is balanced by the fact that if I pass Two Hearts, West may repeat his spades, which will probably suit our side better. Finding little to choose between Three Clubs and a pass, I mark the alternatives:

2NT	10
Pass	5
Three Clubs	5

Reflections on the Bidding

In actual play South passed Two Hearts and sustained a heavy penalty. When the problem was put to a group of experts, who did not know the result, the majority supported the pass. One dissenting critic observed that players who passed Two Hearts either had not realized that this must be bad or were displaying a self-destructive determination to go down with the ship.

PART FIVE

Competitive Decisions

These are mostly competitive hands at the part-score or game level where a decision has to be made whether to pass, double, or bid on. The standard approach, as seen in the first example, is to form an estimate of how many tricks each side is likely to make in its own contract and then to evolve a tactical plan.

42. Off Balance

My opponents in a match-point pairs tournament are enterprising players. With the opposition vulnerable, my partner deals and opens **Three Spades.** East passes and I contemplate:

$$\spadesuit J975 \quad \heartsuit K87 \quad \diamondsuit A9842 \quad \clubsuit 5$$

If only for defensive reasons, I must raise to **Four Spades.** West asks for a review of the bidding and studies the duplicate board, as players do when caught off balance. Eventually he **doubles,** North passes and East bids **Five Clubs.** Now, do I press on? The bidding has been:

South	West	North	East
—	—	3♠	Pass
4♠	Double	Pass	5♣
?			

The Alternatives

If I decide to sacrifice I can go to Five Spades at once or bid Five Diamonds on the way in order to put partner more in the picture. On the other hand, it might be a mistake to sacrifice, and perhaps I should pass or even double. If so, the alternatives are:

Five Spades
Five Diamonds
Double
Pass

The Choice

At this point of a competitive auction I like to consider first, "Who is likely to make what?" and second, "What can I do about it?"

As for our own side, the average expectation of tricks opposite an opening Three bid is about nine, I would say.

Our prospects in defence are harder to calculate. Generally speaking, holding only an Ace and a King plus length in the suit in which partner has pre-empted, I wouldn't expect to defeat an opposing contract at the Five level. However, I mustn't lose sight of the fact that the opponents have not had much time in which to exchange information. West's double was no doubt intended to be optional, and East's Five Clubs may not suit him particularly well. Opponents who contest against a pre-empt don't always land on their feet.

If I had to make the final decision over Five Clubs I would go to Five Spades, but partner is still there and I feel I ought not to prejudge the issue.

There is another reason for letting them play Five Clubs, assuming that partner does not defend. This may not be the only game they can make and Five Clubs may not produce a good score in match points. There is no guarantee that *every* North player will open Three Spades, and some East-West pairs may have a clear run to a game in hearts or even no trump.

Wrong to Double

There is no point in doubling Five Clubs, for if we can beat it we shall make a good score anyway. Also, while I am not going to sacrifice, I must not discourage my partner from doing so.

Five Diamonds or Five Spades?

As between Five Diamonds and Five Spades, Five Diamonds might assist partner to take the right decision should opponents go to Six Clubs. I don't think that is very important here, because unless we could beat Six Clubs we would get a bad score in any event. A sacrifice in spades at the level of Six would be too high in comparison with most other tables.

There is a somewhat better reason for bidding Five Spades rather than Five Diamonds. This is that the higher call gives West less room for manoeuvre. Over Five Diamonds, West can make a forcing pass, he can double, or he can introduce hearts on a suit such as A Q J x x. If Five Spades is bid immediately, West will have a sharper decision.

However, this discussion is academic because I don't propose to make either call in front of my partner. I mark the alternatives:

Pass 10
Five Spades 6
Five Diamonds 4
Double 1

Reflections on the Bidding

When this problem was put to a panel of experts, the majority vote was for bidding on, several critics making the point mentioned above that Five Diamonds would assist partner to judge his action over Six Clubs. As I see it, these answers overlook the practical point that when opponents have begun the exchange of information at the Five level, and especially when there has been an optional double, they often arrive in the wrong spot.

Suppose that the auction had been instead:

South	*West*	*North*	*East*
—	—	3♠	4♣
4♠	5♣	Pass	Pass
?			

Now the presumption that East-West are in their best contract is much stronger, and at the vulnerability the natural action for South would be to sacrifice.

43. Defending at a High Level

In a team event both sides are vulnerable and I am last to speak. My hand is:

♠ A Q J 6 ♡ — ◇ K Q 7 5 4 2 ♣ A 6 4

After two passes East opens with **Four Hearts.** This is one of the situations everybody dislikes:

South	West	North	East
—	Pass	Pass	4♡
?			

The Alternatives

The possibilities include a suit overcall, either Four Spades or Five Diamonds; a take-out request, 4NT or Five Hearts; and a double. Despite the hazards involved in any of these actions, I doubt whether anyone would pass. The alternatives are therefore:

Five Hearts
Five Diamonds
4NT
Four Spades
Double

The Choice

Over a pre-empt of Four Hearts the usual meaning of the artificial or semi-artificial overcalls is as follows:

4NT is for a take-out, with emphasis on the minor suits since Four Spades has been by-passed.

Double is in principle for penalties, but as 4NT tends to deny spades, a double suggests tolerance of that suit.

Five Hearts, an overcall in the opponent's suit, proclaims a very strong two-suiter, probably spades and one of the minors.

Against this background we can consider the merits of the various calls, taking the natural overcalls first.

Four Spades

Obviously a rather wild shot in the dark that might be calamitous. It is true that I could run to Five Diamonds if doubled, but good opponents don't double at this level just because they hold five trumps to the King. They play possum unless they can double any rescue bid.

Five Diamonds

This can't be a bad bid. At least the odds are that we would be in the best suit.

Five Hearts

This would surely be excessive. My hand is not so marvellous that I can force the bidding beyond two of our most likely contracts, Four Spades and Five Diamonds.

Double

There are two points to commend a double. One is that we may well defeat Four Hearts, the other that Four Spades is not ruled out. Partner will not make that bid on 10 x x x but quite possibly he will on:

(1) ♠ K 10 x x x ♡ J x x ◇ x x ♣ K J x

His holding in hearts will suggest to him that I have not doubled mainly on trump tricks.

4NT

This will work well if partner takes out into spades or diamonds. If the response is Five Clubs I will bid Five Diamonds and there will be an inference then that I am interested in spades as well (since with a one-suited hand I would not bid 4NT). Thus, he will transfer to Five Spades on:

(2) ♠ K 10 9 x ♡ Q x x ◇ x ♣ Q J x x x

In this case we would be happier in Four Spades, it is true. That is the disadvantage of 4NT.

Summing Up

We can narrow the issue by crossing out Five Hearts and Four

Spades. Also, Five Diamonds must be inferior to 4NT because on hand (2) above we can find our way to Five Spades, whereas partner would have to pass Five Diamonds.

As between 4NT and double, my feeling is that 4NT, giving us the chance to play in Five Diamonds or Five Spades, will lead to a satisfactory result more often than a penalty double. It is true that we lose the opportunity to play in Four Spades, but that will seldom be achieved unless we plunge straight into it. Partner may take out the double on a five-card spade suit but not on K x x x.

A double will be bad if they make it or if they go down one when we could have made a game. As that will often be the situation, I mark the alternatives:

> 4NT 10
> Five Diamonds 8
> Double 6
> Four Spades 3
> Five Hearts 1

Reflections on the Bidding

Defence to opening bids of Four is one of the most difficult and also neglected parts of the game. In *Blueprint for Bidding* (*The Acol System Today*) a distinction is made between the defences to Four Spades, Four Hearts, and Four of a minor.

One of my general theories is that at this level players try too hard to find the sort of fit that is good enough when the breaks are normal but not when there has been an adverse pre-empt. Thus in the present example you might find partner with 9 x x x in spades and J 10 alone in diamonds and be much better off playing in diamonds. When in doubt, put your trust in the long suit!

44. A Cheerful Prospect

Playing rubber bridge with a sound partner against average opponents I hold in fourth position:

♠ — ♡ A 8 7 4 ◇ A K J 9 7 5 4 ♣ J 3

Neither side is vulnerable and West, on my left, opens **One Heart.** My partner overcalls with **One Spade** and East bids **Two Hearts.** I have to find a strategic call after this sequence:

South	West	North	East
—	1♡	1♠	2♡
?			

The Alternatives

I could bid a number of diamonds from Three to Five. I could double Two Hearts and I might step out with 3NT. That seems to be all, so the alternatives are:

Five Diamonds
Four Diamonds
Three Diamonds
3NT
Double

The Choice

Although I am void in the suit my partner has called, there are hopeful prospects. We might catch them for a penalty in hearts or we might score a surprise game.

A Double Premature

I shall look for a move that retains at any rate one of those possibilities. The first call to reject is a double. That would be decidedly premature. We might set them one trick, though even that is not certain, and we would be missing the chance of better things.

Diamond Raises

Five Diamonds would not be a bad gamble on the values held. Partner is presumably short of hearts and can reasonably be expected to have some support for diamonds. However, my hand contains only eight playing tricks in diamonds, counting no losers in the trump suit. If we can make eleven tricks, partner should be able to raise Four Diamonds to Five. Four Diamonds expresses the value more accurately, and the possibility remains that West, with some sort of heart-club two-suiter, will bid Four Hearts.

Three Diamonds has a better chance of attracting competition, though probably not beyond the range of Three. If Three Diamonds is passed out I shall make overtricks; perhaps too many.

A Fair Gamble

There remains 3NT, a call that becomes more attractive as one examines it. If the diamonds are solid, then nine tricks at no trump should be easier than eleven in diamonds. Partners don't always have the singleton heart you look for, and against Five Diamonds the opponents may lead an early trump.

I must think what might happen after 3NT. Well disciplined partners seldom take back into Four Spades after this sort of sequence, but if he does that I shall have to go Five Diamonds. On the other hand, partner might take out into Four Clubs on a black two-suiter; then he should subside over Four Diamonds. Finally, I expect 3NT to be doubled by East on the strength of his spade holding. If that happens I shall give him the lash with a redouble.

Having persuaded myself that this is a promising venture, I mark the alternatives:

3NT	10
Four Diamonds	6
Three Diamonds	6
Five Diamonds	4
Double	1

Reflections on the Bidding

The problem here is not so much to recognize the merits of 3NT as to think of the call in the first place. Such a bid after the opponents have opened often has a surprise effect. 3NT redoubled and made with an overtrick is not at all an unlikely outcome at rubber bridge!

45. From Four Sides

Playing rubber bridge with a partner who is not shy in competitive situations, I hold as dealer:

♠ K 7 4   ♡ J 10 4 3   ◇ 10 8 2   ♣ K Q 10

With neither side vulnerable, I pass and West, on my left, opens **One Spade.** My partner overcalls with **Two Diamonds** and East comes in with **Two Hearts.** What action, if any, should I take after the bidding has gone:

South	West	North	East
Pass	1♠	2◇	2♡
?			

The Alternatives

I have the values for a raise in diamonds and perhaps for 2NT. Three Clubs, to attract an advantageous opening lead, is a tactical possibility. As opponents are in a forcing position, the best move for the present might be to pass. Nothing else appears plausible, so the alternatives are:

Three Diamonds
Three Clubs
2NT
Pass

The Choice

To say that one has the values for 2NT is one thing; to say that one expects to make it is another. I have a stop of sorts in both their suits, and if West obligingly led away from the Ace of spades and the diamonds were solid I might make several tricks. It is theoretically possible for partner to hold:

♠ x x x   ♡ x   ◇ A Q J 9 x x   ♣ A x x

Even then, if West led a heart, a spade return through my King would be disastrous. I think it would be foolish to press for game at no trump. With an Aceless hand like mine there is seldom time to develop nine tricks.

Unwise to Compete

Three Diamonds is a different proposition to the extent that we might well make it. My club honors should be useful. However, there are several points that can be raised against immediate competition:

(a) Opponents have not so far found a good fit. They may be on their way to a contract they cannot make.

(b) My hand is primarily defensive in type and I certainly don't want to encourage partner to sacrifice at a higher level.

(c) Opponents are in a forcing position. I can pass now and compete on the next round if West calls Two Spades and that is passed to me.

(d) If I bid Three Diamonds now and West becomes declarer at spades, partner may make an unfortunate lead such as Ace of diamonds from A Q.

Three Clubs for a Lead?

This last possibility could be averted by my calling Three Clubs now instead of Three Diamonds. Such a call is often good tactics when one is certain that the opponents will bid on, but here I might well be left to play in a silly contract.

Virtue in a Pass

Having criticized the other calls we remain with a pass, and that does indeed seem to be the best action. I can bid later over Two Spades without any fear lest partner continue the defence at an inauspicious level. Three Diamonds is best of the other calls because if it buys the contract it has a fair chance of being made. I mark the alternatives:

Pass........................10
Three Diamonds.............. 6
2NT 3
Three Clubs................. 3

Reflections on the Bidding

Can you, without looking back, recall the four arguments put forward against the immediate raise to Three Diamonds? They represent useful lines of thought when a close competitive decision as to be made.

Note: Suppose that South passes, as we suggest, and the bidding takes this course:

South	West	North	East
Pass	1♠	2♢	2♡
Pass	2♠	Pass	Pass

Now should South reopen with 2NT or with Three Diamonds?

2NT is better because it leaves partner with more scope for judgment. If he has something like Q x x in spades he will pass 2NT, but if he has a singleton he will remove it.

46. The Pressure Call

In a pairs contest our side is vulnerable and my partner deals and opens **One Diamond.** East passes and my hand is:

♠ A J 6 5   ♡ K J 8 6 4   ◇ 8 3   ♣ J 7

I respond **One Heart** and West comes in with **One Spade.** North bids **Two Diamonds** and East **Two Spades.** It seems a delicate question how far we should go in this part-score battle after the sequence:

South	West	North	East
—	—	1◇	Pass
1♡	1♠	2◇	2♠
?			

The Alternatives

To bid at all on my hand might transfer a plus score into a minus, so there is a case for passing. I could be bolder and double Two Spades. The two most likely forms of positive action are 2NT or a raise in diamonds. To repeat the hearts at the Three level would be unthinkable, so the alternatives appear to be:

> Three Diamonds
> 2NT
> Double
> Pass

The Choice

I will begin by applying my first test on close competitive hands. On the evidence to date, who is likely to make what?

If Two Spades were passed out, I would expect it to go down one or two tricks. If I double, they won't be down more than one. Either way is worth 100 and will not produce a good score if we can make Three Diamonds or 2NT.

Next, what are our prospects in diamonds? If the bidding by our side had been simply One Diamond—One Heart—Two Diamonds, I would have passed and expected North to make it. In the present sequence North has made a free rebid over One Spade, and we are vulnerable, so he must have better than a minimum opening and probably a good six-card suit. He is likely to have a singleton spade on the bidding. Two hearts and four clubs might make up his hand, but that is mostly guesswork.

A contract of Three Diamonds might depend on finesses, but on the whole I would expect it to make. My Jack of clubs may well be a useful card.

I am rather less sanguine about 2NT. I can imagine a spade lead to the Queen forcing my Ace, and then I would have to take tricks quickly. I reckon that if the cards lie well enough for 2NT, Three Diamonds will also be on, but the converse by no means applies.

Having formed this general picture of the prospects in various contracts we are in a better position to study the tactical merits of the various calls.

Pass

Not a mistake, and in a different setting—say at rubber bridge with a less-than-expert partner—it would be the soundest course. Partner is still there and may be able to contend further; if he does not, then Two Spades will probably be defeated. However, in a pairs contest one has to press on these borderline hands, and to accept 50 points or so could be a poor result.

2NT

This presents a fair picture, it might be made, and partner can always take back to Three Diamonds or possibly try Three Clubs. A slight disadvantage to the call is that it warns opponents not to contest with Three Spades—and if they do, they will know where the cards are.

Double

Much too close for my liking, and it violates the general principle that one should not start to double opponents until one has gone to the limit in one's own suits. If opponents were vulnerable, so that a one-trick penalty would be worth 200, the double, though still risky, would stand to gain much more.

Three Diamonds

The disadvantage of this call on the surface is that it might go down when we could have defeated Two Spades. However, it is arguable that if the cards lie badly for us in diamonds they will lie well for the opponents in spades. Three Diamonds has the advantage over 2NT in that it is more likely to stimulate competition. An opponent who has three diamonds may judge that his partner has a singleton and may be disappointed. If East-West go to Three Spades we will have a good chance of doubling them for 300, a relevant point being that a double at that stage would not reveal the trump holding in the same way as a double at the range of Two.

Some of the other calls are not bad, but Three Diamonds is the "pressure bid," and I mark the alternatives:

> Three Diamonds 10
> 2NT 6
> Pass 5
> Double 2

Reflections on the Bidding

The suggested bid of Three Diamonds here may seem to run contrary to the general advice not to be too competitive on primarily defensive hands. That advice holds good only when it is clear that your side is going to be outbid at the finish—that the hand "belongs" to the opponents. Suppose that in this example South's hand had been:

♠ 10 x   ♡ Q 10 x x x   ◇ K x x   ♣ J 9 x

The bidding has gone the same way:

South	West	North	East
—	—	1◇	Pass
1♡	1♠	2◇	2♠
?			

Now Three Diamonds, though likely to go down one or two, is not immediately dangerous because opponents, lacking a trump trick, will scarcely be in a position to double. The bid is pointless, however, because you cannot expect your side to contest the hand to advantage.

By bidding Three Diamonds you simply help the enemy to judge their prospects better.

Reverting to the original hand, a possible criticism of Three Diamonds is that it might encourage partner to bid Four Diamonds over Three Spades. However, a good partner would make that bid in front of you only if he were sure of his ground; and if the bid of Three Spades came on your right, you would be in first with a double.

47. They May Miscalculate

Playing rubber bridge at a table where all the players are competent and aggressive, I hold in fourth position:

♠ Q J 6 2   ♡ 8 6 5 4   ◇ A K 4 3   ♣ Q

With neither side vulnerable West, on my left, opens **One Heart**. My partner overcalls with **Two Clubs** and East raises to **Two Hearts**. I have a useful hand but nowhere very obvious to go after the sequence:

South	West	North	East
—	1♡	2♣	2♡
?			

The Alternatives

I can join in with Two Spades, and a raise in clubs is not out of the question. Three Diamonds, no! I might bid Three Hearts, intending to pass Four Clubs. If none of these appeals, the choice will be between a pass and a double. Any of the following might find supporters:

Three Hearts
Three Clubs
Two Spades
Double
Pass

The Choice

Once again, in approaching a competitive problem the first step is to enquire who is likely to make what. Since there has been an opening bid and a raise against us and I hold 12 points, it is reasonable to assume that a good club suit is the basis for partner's overcall— perhaps A J 10 x x x in clubs plus the King or Ace of spades. My singleton Queen is adequate support for a suit bid at the Two level, and I would expect to make about nine tricks in clubs.

What about a spade contract ? The fact that partner has not doubled does not exclude his holding a 4-1-2-6 hand on which Four Spades might be playable. It's not likely, but it's possible.

As for the chances of the opponents in hearts, all I can say is that my hand appears to be useful defensively. They could have shape I don't know about, but if I had to guess at this moment I would say that we could beat Two Hearts by one trick.

Having reached these few tentative conclusions we can consider the tactical elements in the situation. Game in spades is one of our objectives; a second, more likely to be realized, is a 300 penalty; failing that, we need not be dissatisfied with a part score. Against this background we can assess the various calls.

Three Hearts

This ham-handed effort will extract a spade call from partner when he holds the necessary cards, but meanwhile it destroys all hope of collecting a penalty, and Four Clubs may be too high.

Double

Surely premature. If partner accepts the double we will probably set them by one trick but there might be a disaster. Also, if we double Two Hearts we won't have a chance to double Three!

Two Spades

This will gain only when partner can raise to Four. If he can raise to Three only, it will be dangerous for me to bid the fourth. This is not the sort of hand that will play well with seven trumps, for after the dummy has been shortened it may prove impossible to run the club suit.

Pass

Not ambitious enough. The bidding will probably stay in Two Hearts, and 50 or 100 is too low a target.

Three Clubs

This bid more or less abandons hope of game in spades but is strong in respect to the other objectives. First, the values are there for a raise of the clubs. Second, Three Clubs is the bid most likely to attract competition. This is partly because it sounds innocuous and also

161

because it may mislead the opponents as to the distribution. A player with three small clubs will assume that his partner has a singleton and may be sadly disappointed. If they go to Three Hearts, a 300 penalty should be within range. Partner may take out the double of Three Hearts if he has a seven-card suit, but in that case Four Clubs should be a make.

By comparison, there is little to be said for any of the other calls and I mark the alternatives:

Three Clubs	10
Two Spades	5
Pass	5
Double	3
Three Hearts	2

Reflections on the Bidding

This question was set by Harold Franklin and myself in the course of a radio quiz, and our answer of Three Clubs did not commend itself either to participants in the studio or to listeners at large. When the problem was later put to a panel of experts, our choice was confirmed by a big majority, all making the point that the raise might cause opponents to misjudge their fit.

Many players underestimate the worth of a singleton honor in support of a presumably strong suit. In a constructive auction, when a suit has been rebid, a singleton Queen is as good support as x x x, and a singleton Jack or 10 should be reckoned as equal to a doubleton.

162

48. They Strike First

In a team event, East, on my right, opens **One Heart.** Neither side is vulnerable, and I hold:

♠ K Q 10 7 5 3   ♡ 8   ◇ 4   ♣ Q J 9 3 2

We play Two Spades as a strong overcall and the suit is not good enough for a pre-empt of Three Spades, so I bid simply **One Spade.** West raises his partner to **Four Hearts** and my partner **doubles.** East passes and I have to judge whether to let the double stand after the sequence:

South	West	North	East
—	—	—	1♡
1♠	4♡	Double	Pass
?			

The Alternatives

I can leave the double in or take it out into Four Spades or Five Clubs. Clearly there is nothing to consider beyond the three alternatives:

> Five Clubs
> Four Spades
> Pass

The Choice

This is the sort of decision that wins or loses matches and it may be helpful to examine the arguments on either side. Players who take out the double reason along these lines:

Partner will assume I have one or two defensive tricks, but my long suits may be worth nothing to him in defence against Four Hearts. On the other hand, Four Spades won't go down badly. If I can find him with one or two important cards such as the Jack of spades, the King of clubs, and an Ace, I may even make it. I expect him to hold

163

high cards rather than trumps for his double, for in a situation where opponents are clearly marked with length in their trump suit, the double is co-operative in principle. He is telling me that he has some "tops" and he expects me to use my judgment in deciding whether to pass or bid Four Spades. Obviously Four Spades is the better proposition.

The vision these players form is of partner holding something like:

(1) ♠ A x ♡ x x x ◇ A 10 x x x ♣ K x x

With this hand opposite, Four Spades would be unlucky to fail and Four Hearts would perhaps go down one trick.

A less optimistic assessment would be that both Four Spades and Four Hearts would be defeated 60 per cent of the time, but that the lesser risk would be to defend in spades.

The argument on the other side runs like this:

I am not altogether happy about the double of Four Hearts, for I realize that they may make it if my partner's values include ♣ A K. However, I don't see that I am in any position to reverse my partner's decision. When I overcall at the level of One I don't promise anything much in the way of defensive tricks and if my partner is short of spades my hand may be useful. I realize he can't have tricks in hearts, but he may have enough trumps to be a nuisance. If his only values were top cards in the side suits, and he had a little support for spades, I would expect him to stretch a point and bid Four Spades with minimum trump support rather than double and warn me against bidding on. At a low level I would take out a double of hearts, but at this level I must trust him and pass.

The pass would certainly be right if North's hand were more of this type:

(2) ♠ x ♡ 10 9 x x ◇ K Q 10 x x ♣ A x x

Now Four Hearts, with the enemy trumps 4-4, would surely be defeated while either Four Spades or Five Clubs our way could be a disaster.

The crucial question is: Which of these two hands is North more likely to hold for his double?

Obviously, hand (2), and that seems to me almost the entire answer. On hand (1) most players would pass. They would hope to defeat Four Hearts but would certainly not want to discourage their partners from defending in Four Spades. An imaginative North might even bid Four Spades, judging that partner must have overcalled on length.

The Case for Five Clubs

Five Clubs is not a likely solution, but let us admit that it could be right if partner had doubled on either of these hands:

(3) ♠ x　♡ A x x　◇ J 10 x x x　♣ A 10 x x

(4) ♠ —　♡ 10 x x x　◇ A x x x x　♣ K 10 x x

However, these examples have to be carefully constructed and on most occasions it would be as well to play in Four Spades as Five Clubs even if partner had more clubs than spades. There is the further point that one can always bid Four Spades and test the reaction before venturing on Five Clubs.

Summing Up

My preference for passing is based on two considerations:

1. Both in the short run and the long run, I don't like to cross partner's intentions when he has a better view of the whole situation than I have.

2. In my experience, there is no reason to be pessimistic about the chances of beating Four Hearts. I hold the black suits, partner is likely to have values in the red suits. If I lead a trump, as I intend to, they may be short of tricks.

To rescue into Four Spades would be, to say the least, untrustful, and to rescue into Five Clubs not far short of desperate. I mark the alternatives:

Pass..........................10
Four Spades.................. 4
Five Clubs 2

There are many players who, especially at rubber bridge, will invariably take out a double when they have a two-suiter like this. A curious fact is that they always strike first in the post-mortem (after losing 300 instead of gaining it) by saying, "I couldn't leave it in when you doubled." They don't seem to see the absurdity of saying, in effect, "If you had passed Four Hearts, expressing no opinion, I would have passed too. When you doubled, indicating that you thought we could beat it, I had to bid Four Spades."

If partner had passed Four Hearts it would not have been unreasonable to defend with Four Spades. When he doubled, that surely should have inclined South to the opposite course.

49. No Return

In a pairs event, with both sides vulnerable, my partner opens **One Club** as dealer and the next player passes. My hand is:

♠ Q 8 4 2   ♡ J 10 2   ◇ A 6 5 4   ♣ Q 7

There are three possible responses—One Spade, One Diamond, and 1NT. I don't like One Spade, because the suit is weak and also because there is a sound theoretical basis to the modern style of responding in the lower-ranking four-card suit on this type of hand. 1NT has the merit of defining the hand with fair accuracy, for 1NT over One Club promises about this degree of strength. If the hand were 4-3-3-3 with the same values, I would bid 1NT, but this hand is playable in both major suits and a normal approach of **One Diamond** therefore seems the best choice.

West overcalls with **One Heart,** North bids **One Spade,** and East bids **Two Hearts.** I have a clear raise to **Two Spades.** West persists with **Three Hearts** and this is passed to me. I have a typical match-point decision after the sequence:

South	West	North	East
—	—	1♣	Pass
1◇	1♡	1♠	2♡
2♠	3♡	Pass	Pass
?			

The Alternatives

If this problem arose in the same form at a dozen tables the field might be evenly divided between passing, doubling, and bidding one more in spades. There is nothing beyond the three alternatives:

Three Spades
Double
Pass

The Choice

This is undoubtedly a close decision and one way to approach it is to study the match-point angle. If we let them play undoubled in Three Hearts and set them one, plus 100 will be inferior to making a part score of 110 or 140. If we double and collect 200, that will be close to a top.

Now let's suppose that they can make nine tricks in hearts. Minus 140 will be worse than losing 100 in Three Spades but better than losing 200 in Three Spades doubled. Three Hearts doubled and made will, of course, be a bottom or a joint bottom.

The main conclusion from this is that the match-point odds are against letting them play undoubled in this borderline contract. If we can defeat them, then by doubling we improve our match-point score perhaps from 40 to 90 per cent. If they make it doubled instead of undoubled, we may get zero instead of 15 per cent.

That is the usual answer in these part-score situations when opponents are vulnerable. One has to live dangerously, and the choice is between doubling and going on to Three Spades.

What Are the Prospects in Spades?

My raise to Two Spades was sound enough. Had our bidding followed the same course without any intervention I would have expected to make nine tricks—insofar as one can estimate on this sort of hand. However, the fact that opponents have bid up to the level of Three, vulnerable, points to uneven distribution. No doubt there are singletons around. Because of that I wouldn't put our chances of Three Spades higher than even.

What Are the Prospects of a Double?

This again is difficult to estimate. The contract may well depend on the finesses. If I had to make a wager on this particular issue I would say that the prospects of beating Three Hearts were also about even, perhaps a little better.

There is, however, one strong point for the double. If I bid Three Spades we can't change our minds and go back to double, but if I double partner still has the option of going to Three Spades. Furthermore, he is well placed to make that decision intelligently. He has heard me bid diamonds and support spades and he knows my general strength within fair limits. He will also take into consideration the fact that match-point scoring militated against a pass. In short, he should be able to judge pretty well whether to let the double stand or to take out into Three Spades. Because of the greater flexibility of a double, I mark the alternatives:

> Double 10
> Three Spades 7
> Pass 4

Reflections on the Bidding

This was essentially a match-point problem. At rubber bridge the sound action would be to pass. At I.M.P. scoring the decision would be affected by the general state of the match.

This problem was set in a French magazine alongside one that on the surface was very similar. Neither side is vulnerable and the bidding has gone:

South	West	North	East
—	—	1♣	Pass
1♠	Pass	2♠	Pass
Pass	3♡	Pass	Pass
?			

South's hand is:

♠ Q 10 8 4   ♡ J 9 2   ◇ A 6 5 4   ♣ Q 3

A double is now less attractive for the following reasons:

(*a*) South has bid only spades, not diamonds and spades. North will therefore have less evidence on which to judge whether to take out, and the defence will be more difficult to play exactly.

(*b*) Opponents are not vulnerable and whether you set them 50 or 100 will not make anything like the same difference to your score as when the issue was between 100 and 200.

(*c*) The fact that you have lost the 10 of hearts and gained the 10 of spades may make a difference. It could mean one trick less in defence against Three Hearts, or one trick more in the play of Three Spades.

50. Double Offering

In a team-of-four match our side is vulnerable and my partner deals. In third position I hold:

♠ A Q 10 9 8   ♡ 7   ◇ 10 9 8   ♣ K Q 7 3

My partner opens **One Diamond** and East overcalls with **Three Hearts**. That doesn't worry me for the moment, as I can bid **Three Spades**. West bids **Four Hearts** and this is followed by two passes, leaving me with a typical competitive decision after the sequence:

South	West	North	East
—	—	1◇	3♡
3♠	4♡	Pass	Pass
?			

The Alternatives

I could try for game in any of three denominations—spades, diamonds, or clubs. By bidding 4NT I might improve our chance of settling in the better minor suit. If it seems difficult to find the right spot, I can double for penalties. The alternatives are:

Five Diamonds
Five Clubs
4NT
Four Spades
Double

The Choice

Although partner has made only one bid, a number of inferences can be drawn about his hand. The most he is likely to have in spades is a singleton or J x, for with x x x or K x he would have bid Four Spades rather than leave me with a difficult decision. On the whole he is more likely to hold a doubleton than a singleton, for with a singleton he might have doubled to emphasize a preference for defence. The opponents sound as though they hold ten hearts between them, so the most likely distributions for partner are 2-2-5-4 and 2-2-6-3.

171

Diamonds the Safest Suit

It is probable at any rate that he has some length in diamonds and I wouldn't expect Five Diamonds to go far wrong.

There cannot be the same confidence in Four Spades. Imagine this hand opposite:

(1) ♠ x x   ♡ Q x   ◇ A Q J x x   ♣ A J x x

In Four Spades I would have to ruff the second heart and the hand would be very awkward to play.

Five Clubs is likely to be bad unless partner holds four of them. He will expect me, coming in at this level, to hold a better suit than K Q x x and will pass on:

(2) ♠ J x   ♡ x x   ◇ A Q x x x x   ♣ A 10 x

Some players with this hand would take out Five Clubs into Five Diamonds, but there is no good reason for doing so. For all partner knows, my shape could be 5-2-1-5.

So far, the vote as between the three suits is clearly for diamonds. Also, I would rather bid Five Diamonds than double, because there is no reason to suppose that the penalty would be more than 300. Better still, however, is to offer the choice between two suits, and perhaps 4NT can do this.

What Would 4NT Mean?

I don't want to become involved in an argument about theory at this point. I will just say that, as I play, 4NT would not be Blackwood here for three reasons: no suit has been agreed; I wouldn't regard the previous bid of Three Spades as necessarily forcing, so I could hardly be making a slam try now; and I don't play Blackwood.

Thus, 4NT is available in this sort of sequence as an unusual no trump telling partner that I want to compete either in diamonds or clubs—not because these are the minor suits precisely, but because they are the suits I must have in mind when I by-pass Four Spades.

Five Clubs will be the better contract when partner holds a 2-2-5-4 hand of this nature:

(3) ♠ J x   ♡ x x   ◇ A K x x x   ♣ A J 10 x

If accepted in the sense I have described, 4NT is the winner and I mark the alternatives:

4NT 10
Five Diamonds 8
Double 5
Four Spades................. 3
Five Clubs 3

Reflections on the Bidding

There are some advanced situations where the unusual no trump can be put to work in a most interesting way. In *Blueprint for Bidding* (*The Acol System Today*) Dormer and I give the following example:

♠ 7   ♡ K 8 2   ◇ A Q 10 6 4 3   ♣ A 7 3

Partner opens One Heart, there is an overcall of One Spade, and you bid Two Diamonds. When the bidding next comes around the opponents are in Four Spades. Instead of placing your trust in Five Hearts or Five Diamonds specifically, you bid 4NT. If you had a minor two-suiter you could bid clubs yourself, so partner can work out that you are willing to compete either in Five Hearts or Five Diamonds.

51. Paper Puzzle

My partner at rubber bridge is an enterprising bidder but not a rash one. We are vulnerable, the opponents not, and in third position I hold:

♠ 9 3   ♡ J 10 4 2   ◇ K Q 6   ♣ 7 5 4 2

My partner opens **One Spade** and East overcalls with **Two Hearts.** I pass this, West raises to **Three Hearts,** and now my partner comes in with **Four Diamonds.** East goes on to **Four Hearts** and I have what seems a close decision to make after the sequence:

South	West	North	East
—	—	1♠	2♡
Pass	3♡	4◇	4♡
?			

The Alternatives

If I decide to support my partner the obvious call is Five Diamonds, but Four Spades might also be playable. With my trump holding I could double Four Hearts. If none of these appeals, I can pass the decision up to my partner. There are four alternatives:

Five Diamonds
Four Spades
Double
Pass

The Choice

The standard question—"Who, on the evidence so far, is likely to make what?"— is difficult to answer here. I imagine that we can defeat Four Hearts by a trick or two, but our prospects in spades or diamonds are by no means clear.

Partner has not opened with a Two bid (as in our system he would with a very powerful two-suiter) but he has bid to the level of Four on his own, vulnerable. No doubt he has ten or eleven cards in spades and diamonds. On the surface, if he is 6-5, the long suit should be spades, but I don't regard that as certain. Players often open One Spade on a hand such as:

(1) ♠ A K J x x   ♡ —   ♢ J 10 8 7 x x   ♣ A x

The fact that partner has bid Four Diamonds, not Three Spades, does suggest that he may hold better diamonds than spades. But no doubt he could also hold:

(2) ♠ A Q J x x x   ♡ x   ♢ A J 10 x x   ♣ x

Now we would have a rather better chance in Four Spades than in Five Diamonds.

If he has only five cards in each suit he will be somewhat stronger, such as:

(3) ♠ A K Q x x   ♡ x   ♢ A J 9 x x   ♣ K x

Assuming that I intend to make either call, it is not easy to decide between Four Spades and Five Diamonds. If partner has only five spades, then a contract of Four Spades will be extremely hazardous unless the spades are as strong as in example (3).

Any spade or diamond contract will fail if the suits break badly. It is probably right to say that if they can make Four Hearts, owing to freakish distribution, we would be doubled and perhaps heavily defeated in either of our contracts.

That seems to be the deciding factor. Take this likely sort of hand for partner:

(4) ♠ A K x x x x   ♡ —   ♢ A J 10 x x   ♣ Q x

If the adverse spades are 3-2 we can make Four Spades, barring an unexpected accident such as a trump promotion. But if the spades are 4-1 we shall still have a good chance to make four tricks in defence. In short, this is not one of those hands on which there might be game for both sides. It is a hand where, if by chance we cannot beat Four Hearts, we shall certainly be down in Four Spades.

Double or Pass?

Though it didn't seem obvious at first, I am fairly clear in my mind now that it would be a mistake to bid either Five Diamonds or Four

175

Spades. I expect to defeat Four Hearts, but I am not sure that I ought to double in front of my partner. If he is 6-1-6-0 or has any powerful hand on which he will be bidding Four Spades if I pass, I am more than content that he should do so. He would have to respect a double on my part, because all my values could be in hearts and clubs. If I pass we may score 100 instead of 300, but if I double we may set them one trick instead of making a game. As it may be wrong to commit our side to a definite course either way, I mark the alternatives:

$$
\begin{aligned}
&\text{Pass} \dotfill 10 \\
&\text{Double} \dotfill 8 \\
&\text{Four Spades} \dotfill 5 \\
&\text{Five Diamonds} \dotfill 5
\end{aligned}
$$

Reflections on the Bidding

When this problem was put to an expert panel, there were 6 votes for Five Diamonds, 5 for Four Spades, and a lone voice (mine, though I now consider a pass to be more accurate) for double.

I have a feeling that these eleven votes for supporting partner were "paper answers." That is to say, at the table, with a sure trump trick and a promising line of defence (the lead should be King of diamonds) many of these players would prefer to defend rather than place such stress on partner's vulnerable bidding.

My own view is that at this level it is usually easier to make four tricks in defence than ten or eleven in attack and that to press on is essentially the "expert's error."

52. The Tale Travelled

In a team event our side is vulnerable and as dealer I hold:

♠ —   ♡ J 7   ◇ Q J 9 8 6 2   ♣ Q 8 7 5 4

After two passes my partner opens **1NT.** We are playing a fairly strong no trump of 16 to 18 points. East overcalls with **Three Spades** and I feel justified in contesting with **Four Diamonds.** West bids **Four Spades,** my partner **doubles,** and East passes. I have an unenviable decision to make after the sequence:

South	West	North	East
Pass	Pass	1NT	3♠
4◇	4♠	Double	Pass
?			

The Alternatives

There are clearly three calls to consider. I can pass the double or take out into one of my minor suits. The alternatives are:

Five Diamonds
Five Clubs
Pass

The Choice

My hand is far from attractive for defence against Four Spades, but before I take any hasty action I must ask myself a few questions. The first is, "Have I misled my partner concerning my defensive values?"

The answer to that is, "No." My bid of Four Diamonds was part-score contesting and my smattering of Queens and Jacks, which will probably add up to one defensive trick, are as much as partner has a right to expect.

The second question is, "Does my 6-5 distribution represent a threat to our defensive prospects?"

177

I cannot answer that with the same confidence. The worst that can happen is that the dummy will go down with J 10 9 x x in clubs and partner's A K x will pull in no tricks at all.

Of course, if the distribution is going to be as bad as that, we may be set 500 in Five Clubs or Five Diamonds doubled, as against 590 for Four Spades doubled and made.

One further question is, "To what extent does partner's double of Four Spades affect the situation?"

With a less-than-expert partner in the North position the double would mean very little. Any average player, having opened a strong no trump and heard his partner bid at the Four level, would automatically double the opponents in Four Spades.

A good player will not reason in that way. If he has just an average no trump with an average holding in spades and diamonds he will say to himself, "Partner has heard me open 1NT vulnerable. As I have nothing special to add I can pass the decision up to him."

Coming from a good player, the double is an express warning that North is better suited to defence against Four Spades than to play in Five Diamonds. My length in clubs introduces another factor, as was noted above, but I still think I ought to heed the warning. He may have —indeed he must have—tricks in the trump suit itself.

Five Clubs Preferable to Five Diamonds

If I were going to bid on, I would call Five Clubs, not Five Diamonds. Five Clubs could not possibly be a slam try, for my hand is limited by the previous Four Diamonds. Partner has told me that he has no good support for diamonds, but he could hold four good clubs. Indeed, the only reason for removing the double would be that I expected to find long clubs opposite.

When I find myself in doubt at this level, I tend, as in the preceding example, to fall back on the general proposition that four tricks are easier to win than eleven, and as that is my feeling here I mark the alternatives:

Pass.........................10
Five Clubs 6
Five Diamonds 4

Reflections on the Bidding

This problem was posed by a player whose team-mate had removed the double and sustained a somewhat excessive penalty of 800. Against Four Spades he would have won four top tricks. Perhaps the tale travelled, for the panel voted 80 per cent for passing the double. I fear that at the table, if the situation could be reproduced for one hundred players, that proportion would just about be reversed.

53. Deceptive Cost

Playing rubber bridge with a partner whom I do not know well but who seems to play a fair game, I hold in fourth position:

$$\spadesuit A K Q 9 8 3 \quad \heartsuit 9 5 \quad \diamondsuit J 10 5 2 \quad \clubsuit 4$$

The opponents are vulnerable and West, on my left, opens **1NT**. They are playing a fairly strong no trump, about 16 to 18 points. North passes and East raises to **3NT**. My spades are still on the shelf, the bidding having gone:

South	West	North	East
—	1NT	Pass	3NT
?			

The Alternatives

I can pass, I can double in the hope of attracting the right lead, or I can defend with Four Spades. There's nothing else to consider, so the alternatives are:

Four Spades
Double
Pass

The Choice

We can begin, as usual, by trying to estimate who is likely to make what. If I sacrificed in Four Spades I would expect to make about eight tricks and so lose, on average, 300. Their prospects may depend on the lead, but even if a spade is not forthcoming there is no certainty that they will make the game. Partner may hold clubs, for example, and by the time he comes in I shall have had a chance to signal.

At duplicate scoring, if you judged that they might well make 3NT, it would be right to sacrifice, but at rubber bridge it is a bad bargain to accept a likely 300 loss defending against a questionable game. Even if I had a guarantee that I would be only down one, I wouldn't sacrifice here.

What Would a Double Mean?

The important question is, would partner interpret a double as a request to make an unusual lead, and would he pick the right suit?

One doesn't double on a scattered 15 points in this position, so it seems logical to treat the double as lead-directing, no doubt based on a suit that one hopes to run. Partner should choose his shortest suit, and if he has equal length in spades and diamonds he should choose the spade lead because when opponents bid to 3NT without any exploring they are more likely to have length in the minors than in the majors.

Balance of Advantage

Assuming for the present that partner will interpret the double as I want him to, let us examine some other aspects and see where the balance of advantage lies.

At best, the double will gain 1,000 points or so, if as a result of the spade lead they go down 500 instead of making the game. (I trust that I don't have to explain to present readers that the value of the second game, including the trick score, is about 500—not the 800 that goes down on the score sheet, for that includes the unseen value of the first game.)

I realize that my spades are not necessarily solid. As West has opened a strong no trump with no top honor in spades, he may have J x x x or an equivalent guard. But even then the spade lead may be a good defence. At least partner will have been deflected from a calamitous lead of a low club from, say, Q 10 x x.

They may redouble. I can consider that when it happens and whence it comes. Retreat to Four Spades will still be available.

With a doubleton spade and a singleton diamond partner may make the wrong choice. Unlucky!

As I said at the beginning, I don't know my partner well and he may not get the message at all. If he makes his natural lead they may end up with three doubled overtricks. Oh well, I shall have a new partner for the next rubber. So will he!

I mark the alternatives:

Double 10
Pass. 5
Four Spades. 2

181

Reflections on the Bidding

One of the commonest mistakes in competitive bidding is to overcall in this sort of situation. When players go off 300 only to find they could have defeated the opponents, they shrug it off with the remark, "I knew it couldn't cost much."

In fact, they have lost 350 or 400 points by bidding on instead of passing or doubling. Had they been right, in that opponents would have made their game, the gain at rubber bridge is only about 200. So before embarking on a sacrifice of this kind, you want to be satisfied that the odds are two to one on their being able to make game.

The idea that the double of 3NT should be lead-directing here may be new to some readers. It is probably a good system to treat all unexpected doubles of game contracts, like the Lightner double of a slam contract, as lead-directing.

54. Dubious Action

In a team event neither side is vulnerable and in fourth position I hold:

♠ 8 5   ♡ K Q 8 7 5   ◇ 3   ♣ A Q J 8 4

West, on my left, opens **One Spade,** my partner passes, and East responds **Two Diamonds.** The question is whether—and if so, how—I should enter the auction after the sequence:

South	West	North	East
—	1♠	Pass	2◇
?			

The Alternatives

I can pass for the moment and decide later whether or not to contest. I can come in with a straightforward Two Hearts, or I can signify my two-suiter by doubling or by bidding 2NT, which partner will take as the "unusual no trump" denoting length in the unbid suits. Thus there are four alternatives:

2NT
Two Hearts
Double
Pass

The Choice

When both opponents have shown signs of strength and I have a useful hand, I like to consider first whether there is any likelihood that our side can obtain the contract, other than by way of an unprofitable sacrifice. There doesn't seem much prospect of that here. There is not room for partner to have more than 6 points or so and those would have to be distributed in an exceptionally lucky way for us to outbid the enemy. He might have support for hearts but they would still have the higher ranking suit.

183

Any action I take will therefore be of a defensive nature. Is it likely that we will have a profitable sacrifice at the Five level against Four Spades? Possibly, but almost surely we would go down 300 to save 420. It is still less likely that it would pay us to sacrifice over 3NT.

We might be able to compete at the level of Three, it is true, but that can be achieved by passing now and reopening if West bids Two Spades and East passes.

Disadvantages of Bidding

It looks as though the advantages of positive action are slight. Are there possible disadvantages? Surely! There are three:

(*a*) You give the opponents a "fielder's choice" between doubling your side or taking a part score or going for game, according to their strength.

(*b*) Should they reach game despite the intervention they will be assisted in the play. This applies particularly if South makes one of the calls denoting a two-suiter—double or 2NT.

(*c*) Whatever form of intervention you select, you will be under strength in some respect and that may cause partner to embark on a costly defence. Thus, if you enter with Two Hearts you suggest a better suit; if with a double, more high cards; if with 2NT, more playing strength.

Best of the Others

Of the three forms of positive action, 2NT is the most dangerous in that it forces your side to the level of Three. If opponents are not happy about their fit they will take the opportunity to double.

Two Hearts has the disadvantage of not telling partner (or the opponents, it is true) that you have equal values in clubs. Also, the suit is weak for intervention in this exposed position. If Two Hearts is doubled you will have an awkward guess whether to retreat to Three Clubs.

A double exaggerates the general quality of the hand, but with this call you have a better chance of escaping a penalty.

Summing Up

I intend to pass, expecting the hand to develop in one of the following ways:

Opponents will bid game or stop just short. Then I shall be glad not to have given them free information about the distribution.

West will bid Two Spades. East will pass. Then I shall have a close decision whether to contest with 2NT, but I can meet that problem when it arises.

West will raise Two Diamonds to Three and East will pass. Then I may regret that I did not enter on the previous round. But that is the only time, and I mark the alternatives:

Pass	10
Double	6
Two Hearts	5
2NT	4

Reflections on the Bidding

The point of this example is to emphasize that it is apt to be a mistake to enter the auction when you have little chance of challenging for the contract. One of the popular modern toys, the unusual no trump, is often misused in that way. Say that at equal vulnerability South holds:

♠ x ♡ x ◇ Q 10 x x x x ♣ A 9 x x x

He passes and West, on his left, opens One Heart. North passes and East responds One Spade. South now thinks, "Ah! Good opportunity to show my distribution! I passed originally so partner will know just what I've got when I bid 1NT."

So he will, but whom will it profit? The opponents, in both the bidding and the play!

55. Mainly Diamonds

Playing in a team-of-four match against first-class opponents, I hold in last position:

♠ 4 ♡ A K J 6 3 ◇ 2 ♣ A Q J 8 6 5

With neither side vulnerable, West deals and opens **Four Spades**. My partner overcalls with **Five Diamonds** and East **doubles**. A lot of points will depend on my action now:

South	West	North	East
—	4♠	5◇	Double
?			

The Alternatives

I can leave partner in Five Diamonds doubled or I can take the initiative and redouble. If I decide to remove the double I can bid one of my suits or perhaps Five Spades, requesting partner to choose between hearts and clubs. The alternatives are:

Six Clubs
Five Spades
Five Hearts
Redouble
Pass

The Choice

If we credit West with most of the spade suit there is not a lot for North and East to hold in the way of high cards. Apart from the diamonds there is only the Queen of hearts and the King of clubs.

Who is likely to hold those two cards—North or East? East, I feel sure, must have some strength outside diamonds, for when an opponent has overcalled at the Five level the partner of the pre-emptive bidder keeps very quiet on a trump holding such as Q 10 9 x x. At any rate, a good player does, and East is certainly that.

What Is Left for North to Hold?

Diamonds and—diamonds! We have come to the heart of the matter very quickly. Moreover, to bid at the Five level with no high cards outside his long suit, North should have seven or eight likely tricks in the suit—not less than A K J 10 x x x or A Q J x x x x x.

What Are Our Chances in Five Diamonds?

We may lose a spade and two diamonds, obviously. But East may have doubled with only one trump trick, expecting to make a diamond, a spade, and another trick somewhere.

Could Another Suit Be Better?

It seems unlikely. Suppose you are lucky enough to find partner with, say, 10 x x x of hearts in addition to his diamonds. Since the diamonds are not going to be solid there will still be work to do even in Five Hearts.

A further objection to any kind of rescue bid is that you cannot be at all sure of making the right one. You could bid Five Hearts and find that you would have been better off in clubs. If you bid Five Spades you will arrive at the better of your suits (unless a furious partner can say only Six Diamonds, which is not unlikely), but meanwhile you have excluded Five Hearts.

Would a Redouble Be a Fair Venture?

The odds are slightly against. The chances of making or going one down may be about equal, but two down must be adjudged more likely than an overtrick. In addition, if opponents run to Five Spades the penalty may be 500, but not more.

Nevertheless I prefer a redouble to a rescue and I mark the alternatives:

Pass........................10
Redouble 5
Five Spades 3
Five Hearts 2
Six Clubs 2

Reflections on the Bidding

The clue to this problem lay in reflecting that East would not have doubled on trump tricks alone; therefore there was nothing for North to hold but a long string of diamonds.

South's decision would have been more difficult if his opponent had been a poor player or if he could have called his longer suit at the level of Five. But even then, with an undisclosed A K and an A Q J and a singleton, should one rescue a partner who has overcalled at the level of Five ? Please don't do it to me!

56. From the Back Seat

In a team-of-four match our side is vulnerable and my partner deals. My hand is:

♠ K ♡ K ◇ Q 10 6 5 3 2 ♣ Q J 9 6 5

Partner opens **One Club** and East **doubles.** The vulnerability is against us but a pre-empt of **Four Clubs** seems a reasonable move. This is passed to East, the original doubler, who now bids **Four Hearts.** I have to think again after the sequence:

South	West	North	East
—	—	1♣	Double
4♣	Pass	Pass	4♡
?			

The Alternatives

There are two ways of bidding on—Five Clubs and, not as obvious, 4NT. If I think I have done enough I can pass or double. The alternatives are:

Five Clubs
4NT
Double
Pass

The Choice

I don't know a lot about the hand so far. My partner has opened the bidding but has passed Four Clubs, and East has refused to be shut out. Whether his Four Hearts was an overbid, or whether he is strong, I have no sure way of telling.

In such circumstances it can hardly be right for me to take a final decision in front of my partner. My hand is not so barren of defensive values that I should say, "They must be able to make Four Hearts and I don't want to hear what anyone else thinks about it." Partner

189

knows more about my hand than I do about his, and therefore he is better placed to judge.

Double or Pass?

The only problem really is whether I should double. It is true that I have no guarantee of defeating Four Hearts, but my defensive values are more than partner will expect from my raise to Four Clubs. The two singleton Kings would have little, if any, value in Five Clubs, but they could be useful cards in defence against Four Hearts. Since my general strength is limited by the previous call of Four Clubs it must be safe, and indeed right, to double. If partner still wants to defend in Five Clubs, that's up to him.

The Meaning of 4NT

I am not proposing to bid 4NT, but the idea behind that call is worth noting. Following the raise to Four Clubs and by-passing Four Spades, its only meaning could be, "I have a long suit of diamonds as well as the club support. Possibly, if we are going to compete, Five Diamonds would be better than Five Clubs." This stratagem would gain when partner held:

$$\spadesuit A x x \quad \heartsuit x x \quad \diamondsuit K J x x \quad \clubsuit A K x x$$

Playing in diamonds there would be less danger of a ruff in the other minor suit. Five Diamonds would also be safer when partner had opened a short club suit and had the same number of diamonds.

4NT has a slight advantage over Five Clubs, therefore, but the distinction is a matter of academic interest, as either call would be a mistake. With an intelligent partner it must be right to double and I mark the alternatives:

Double	10
Pass	7
4NT	3
Five Clubs	2

Reflections on the Bidding

The problem arose in a European Championship match between Britain and Austria. Adam Meredith's judgment in doubling was rightly admired. Four Hearts doubled was down two and there would have been no play for Five Clubs.

The approach to South's bid on the second round should be, "Who can judge this situation better—my partner or myself?" The answer, clearly, is partner, for South has already given a good picture of his holding. To bid Five Clubs in front of partner would be a prime example of the malady I describe as "back-seat driving."

PART SIX

Protective Situations

Most partnerships have their own ideas concerning the values for, and meaning of, bids in the protective position. Here we look at a few examples where the sensible call has to be chosen without reference to system agreement.

57. No Surprise

In a team event the opponent on my right deals and opens **One Spade.** Both sides are vulnerable and I hold:

♠ A 6 2   ♡ A 10 7 4 3   ◇ A 9 4   ♣ 7 2

Either a double or an overcall of Two Hearts would be dangerous on this primarily defensive hand, so I pass. West passes also, and my partner reopens with **Two Clubs.** East bids **Two Spades** and I have to assess the worth of my hand after the sequence:

South	West	North	East
—	—	—	1♠
Pass	Pass	2♣	2♠
?			

The Alternatives

On the strength of my three Aces I could bid 2NT or even 3NT. If I take the view that East's vulnerable rebid casts a blight over the prospects of game at no trump I can introduce Three Hearts or support my partner's clubs on the doubleton. I might decide that we could beat Two Spades and chance a double. Three Spades (asking partner to bid 3NT if he had a spade stop) would generally take the bidding too high, while a pass would be too feeble, so the alternatives are:

3NT
2NT
Three Hearts
Three Clubs
Double

The Choice

East is vulnerable, he has heard his partner pass, yet he has bid Two Spades when very much under the gun. He will surely have at least six spades and probably a trick in clubs. In that case even 2NT will be too much.

However, I suppose it is possible for East to have a strongly distributed hand without a top card in clubs. He could have something in the nature of:

♠ K Q J 9 x x   ♡ x   ♢ K Q 10 x x   ♣ x

He would bid Two Spades on this to make it more difficult for opponents to get together in hearts.

But if I place East with that sort of hand, West may be so annoying as to turn up with K x x x or Q 10 x x in clubs. We may still have difficulty in making nine tricks.

It is true that partner can sign off in Three Clubs over 2NT, but on many hands he will have no reason to do so and 2NT will go down.

The only other approach to game is by way of Three Hearts. It is possible for partner to hold K J x of hearts or even better, but the odds must be strongly against his being able to bid Four Hearts. Even Three Hearts will be a hopeless contract if West holds most of the outstanding length.

Would a Double Be Sound?

The remaining aggressive action is to double Two Spades on the grounds that our side must have the balance of the high cards, that East will never be able to enter dummy, and so forth. Against that, there are hundreds of strongly distributed hands on which East will have no difficulty in making eight tricks. It is not as though my hand contained any nasty surprise for him. He *knows* he hasn't got the three Aces!

Is There Any Merit in Three Clubs?

More than in any of the other calls we have examined. You can expect to make it because there is not much for partner to hold other than reasonably good clubs. It must be better to contest the part score safely than to try for a game that has about one chance in four of succeeding. I mark the alternatives:

Reflections on the Bidding

If this bid of Three Clubs strikes some readers as peculiar or worse, the mote is in their own eyes. I am fortified in that judgment by the fact that when the problem was put to an expert panel, with the Jack of diamonds added in place of the 9, the vote for Three Clubs was almost unanimous.

The argument relating to a double of Two Spades is worth noting. South's approach should not be, "How can they make eight tricks against the weight of cards we hold?" Instead he should reflect, "East evidently thinks he won't go far wrong in Two Spades. What is there in my hand that will come as an unpleasant surprise to him?" The answer to that, obviously, is "Nothing."

58. How Will It Play?

With both sides vulnerable in match play, the bidding is opened on my right with **One Heart.** My hand is:

♠ A   ♡ 8 6 4 3 2   ◇ A J 5 3   ♣ A K J

I don't like trap passes if there is a reasonable alternative, but here I can see none. I pass and so does West. My partner protects with **One Spade** and the opener passes. I have to find an intelligent call after this sequence:

South	West	North	East
—	—	—	1♡
Pass	Pass	1♠	Pass
?			

The Alternatives

If you put this problem to ten players you might get ten different answers, ranging from a pass to 3NT.

Two Diamonds and Three Diamonds are possibilities. You could take the view that the hand should play well in spades and so raise despite the singleton. You could give it up as hopeless and let him play One Spade. You might try to express the hand by bidding some quantity of no trump. If we look no further, the list will read:

Four Spades
Three Spades
Two Spades
3NT
2NT
1NT
Three Diamonds
Two Diamonds
Pass

I have not included Two Hearts because that might be interpreted as showing a heart suit. Being short in hearts himself, partner would be all the more likely to pass.

The Choice

Let's begin by considering what partner is likely to hold and whether there is any chance of game. Allowing for East's vulnerable opening, there is not much left for North to hold, apart from fair spades and one or two high cards in the minor suits. These are some minimum examples:

(1) ♠ K J x x x x ♡ x ◇ Q x ♣ x x x x

(2) ♠ K J 10 x x ♡ x ◇ 10 9 x x ♣ Q x x

(3) ♠ Q J 9 x x ♡ x x ◇ K Q x ♣ 10 x x

I would not expect him to protect on less than this. Some players do, but that is not our style.

What strikes me at once is that even these moderate hands offer a play for game. Take hand (1), played in spades. Declarer would not draw trumps, of course. After a heart lead he would play to make all the trumps in his hand by ruffing. If he could cash four tricks in the minors, that would be enough.

Little Chance for 3NT

Even if we agree that game is possible we still have to get there in co-operative fashion. Which bids can we strike out? All no trump bids, I would say. Apart from the fact that the puny aggregation in hearts may not amount to a stop, we may be cut off from partner's spades. We shall land on our feet only if the spades are rebid.

Simple bids such as Two Spades and Two Diamonds are harmless but will lead nowhere, for it is most unlikely that partner will have enough to continue. It would be simpler to pass and make sure of a plus score that way.

Four Spades, though not so peculiar as it may look, would be unduly precipitous. If partner held hand (3) above, the defence would begin with three rounds of hearts on which West would shed minor suit losers, and Four Spades would be down at least one, probably more.

There remain for consideration Three Diamonds and Three Spades.

What Would Three Diamonds Mean?

Not long diamonds, surely. With a suit such as A K Q x x x and other values to justify the jump, I would have overcalled on the first round.

Nor will partner take Three Diamonds to conceal strong support for spades, for with good trump support I would raise directly.

I think he would judge that my spade support was limited, but that I hoped for game in either spades or diamonds. He might place me with a hand of this kind:

♠ K x ♡ K 9 x x ◇ A K J x x ♣ x x

With these defensive values I might pass the opening One Heart and it would be natural to follow with Three Diamonds. If he formed that sort of picture he would presumably jump to Four Spades if he had a good suit, and if he could raise diamonds he would do so. If he could say no more than Three Spades I would pass. This seems a fair solution.

What of Three Spades?

I make this a clear second best. With a less-than-expert partner—one who would not draw the right inferences from Three Diamonds—it would be the first choice.

Assuming a first-class partner, I mark the alternatives as follows:

Three Diamonds	10
Three Spades	7
Four Spades	4
Pass	4
Two Spades	4
Two Diamonds	3
1NT	2
2NT or 3NT	1

With a moderate player opposite, Three Spades would be wiser than Three Diamonds, and the unambitious calls—Two Spades, Two Diamonds, and pass—would move up.

Reflections on the Bidding

This problem has been considered by expert panels on both sides of the Atlantic. Many judges said that it was insoluble. Certainly, one cannot be sure of obtaining the best result, but the problem begins to straighten out when one realizes:

That the hand should play well in spades. Even with a five-card suit North might be able to land Four Spades by way of five trumps and five tricks in the minor suits.

That Three Diamonds should secure from an expert partner the desired reaction—either a sign-off in Three Spades, a jump to Four Spades, a raise of diamonds, or conceivably 3NT.

59. Information Withheld

In a pairs event, playing against opponents who will not miss any chances, I am fourth to speak and hold:

♠ A 9 5 2   ♡ 8   ◇ A K 7 6   ♣ Q 10 7 3

Neither side is vulnerable and after two passes the bidding is opened on my right with **One Spade.** For the moment I can only pass. West responds with **1NT,** and two passes follow. I have to decide whether to compete after this sequence:

South	West	North	East
—	Pass	Pass	1♠
Pass	1NT	Pass	Pass
?			

The Alternatives

I can go quietly and pass. If I compete, the possibilities are double or an overcall in one of the minors. The alternatives are therefore:

Two Diamonds
Two Clubs
Double
Pass

The Choice

When opponents are in 1NT and I am wondering whether to protect in any way, I find it useful to ask myself these questions:

Is there any reason to suppose that our side has the balance of the cards?

Even if we have not, can I compete with reasonable safety and also with some purpose?

The answer to the first question on this occasion is plainly negative.

All I know so far is that East has opened the bidding and West has responded. East could be close to maximum for his pass and West could have a fairly strong no trump. They could have up to 24 points between them. True, East could also have made a semi-psychic opening, but I have no reason to assume that.

At any rate, it is plain that it would be dangerous to double. We might find outselves defending 1NT doubled with inferior cards or partner might end up as declarer in Two Hearts doubled and lose 300 on a part-score deal.

If I defend in one of the minors I have a better chance of escaping alive. If I bid Two Clubs, West may not have enough trumps to double or he may bid Two Hearts before giving his partner a chance. If Two Clubs is promptly doubled I can transfer to Two Diamonds. After that I might even run to Two Spades.

What Are the Possible Advantages of Competing?

The prospect of scoring 90 in Two Clubs instead of losing 90 or 120 in 1NT is slight even if partner has support for clubs. The opponents will surely contest in turn with Two Spades or Two Hearts.

Suppose, finally, that East is psychic, that partner has 9 or 10 points, and that we beat them in 1NT. Will it be a tragedy that we have not doubled? Not at all! Plus 100 won't be a bottom score.

Actually the best reason for competing is the singleton heart and the prospect of an unfortunate lead against 1NT. That does give some ground for seeking to introduce a diversion. I mark the alternatives:

Pass..........................10
Two Clubs................... 5
Two Diamonds 3
Double 3

Reflections on the Bidding

This was not a deep question, and many readers will say that the pass is obvious. I assure them, nevertheless, that many players would compete, not only in a pairs and not vulnerable, but at I.M.P. scoring and vulnerable. 1NT doubled and made with an overtrick is one of the commonest results in tournament play.

When you have upward of 13 points and both opponents are in the bidding against you, the only inference you are entitled to draw is that your partner has very little! The best tactical course is to pass 1NT without letting the opponents realize that you have anything to think about. The declarer will almost always drop a trick in the play, not expecting the adverse strength to be so unevenly divided.

60. No Need to Worry

On the first deal of a rubber I am last to speak and hold:

♠ A Q 8 3   ♡ A 7 4   ◇ 6   ♣ A K Q 6 5

To my disappointment, the bidding is opened on my left with **One Spade.** This is followed by two passes. I have to bid in the protective position after the sequence:

South	West	North	East
—	1♠	Pass	Pass
?			

The Alternatives

The orthodox manoeuvre on such a strong hand is to double. Three Clubs is a possibility and I must consider a jump to 2NT. If none of those calls seems likely to lead anywhere I can pass and pick up an easy 100 or so. The alternatives are:

Three Clubs
2NT
Double
Pass

The Choice

If opponents were vulnerable it would be reasonable to let them stew in One Spade, for whether we can make a game is doubtful. A non-vulnerable penalty of 100 odd hardly seems enough—we could be certain of that much by bidding a tame 1NT or Two Clubs. Thus, a pass need not be seriously considered.

Where a Double Is Unsatisfactory

What I have to look for is a sequence that will not take us too high if partner has nothing and will give us a chance to reach game if he has a few points in the right place. I am not sure that a double will achieve

203

that. If partner responds Two Hearts I shall have to take a chance and bid game in hearts, for neither 2NT nor Three Hearts would evoke a response. Over Two Diamonds I would presumably bid 2NT, but again that would not express my strength. To double in the protective position and follow with 2NT over a response at the Two level is often correct on 15 points or so, and here I have 19 with a strong suit.

3NT the Most Likely Game Spot

An immediate 2NT will sound stronger and I think that may well be the best answer. Partner will raise this on the 5 points or so that I need for game.

It is true that if I bid 2NT partner will not feel called upon to show a moderate suit of hearts. But will that matter? It will seldom happen that he can make ten tricks in hearts, with the lead coming through my spades, while I can make only eight at no trump.

Three Clubs Too Weak

If I could get a free bid from partner over Three Clubs there would be no problem. The trouble is that I could bid Three Clubs on so much less—a strong six-card suit and a side Ace. With a smattering of high cards in diamonds—all I want for 3NT—partner will not respond.

To double and bid Three Clubs on the next round would reflect the strength better than bidding Three Clubs immediately. It would seldom lead to 3NT, however, and I mark the alternatives:

$$
\begin{array}{ll}
\text{2NT} & 10 \\
\text{Double} & 6 \\
\text{Three Clubs} & 5 \\
\text{Pass} & 3 \\
\end{array}
$$

Reflections on the Bidding

Bidding in the protective position on a strong hand generally needs thought because of the relative lack of bidding space. The situation here was that South could not justifiably gamble on a game without some forward move by his partner. To double and then bid 2NT over partner's response at the level of Two would not be sufficient to prompt that move.

204

Had the setting of the suits been different a double would have been correct. Thus, suppose that the opening bid had been One Club and South had held:

♠ A x x   ♡ x   ♢ A K Q x x   ♣ A Q x x

Now he can double and make a *jump* bid of 2NT over the expected response of One Heart. That expresses the hand well enough.

Some players, with the original hand, would give no thought to no trump because of the singleton diamond. With a strong suit, and the other controls, one does not have to worry too much about a singleton. If the worst (or nearly worst) happens and the opponents run the first five tricks in your short suit, you simply discard from your less valuable holdings and wait for the weather to brighten.

61. Unreliable Guide

Both sides are vulnerable in a pairs event. In third position I hold:

♠ 5 3 2   ♡ 9 7 2   ◇ 6 4 2   ♣ A K 7 4

My partner opens **One Heart** and East overcalls **One Spade**. I don't hold free bids in special awe and if I thought this hand was worth a raise I would produce it, but such virtue as it possesses is more of a defensive nature and I am content to pass. West passes and my partner reopens with a **double**. East passes and the question is whether I should make a constructive call now after the sequence:

South	West	North	East
—	—	1♡	1♠
Pass	Pass	Double	Pass
?			

The Alternatives

The possible responses fall into two divisions—the minimum bids (Two Clubs and Two Hearts), and the stronger bids (Three Clubs and Three Hearts). Another possibility in the latter group is a bid of the opponent's suit. To pass the double, hoping to score 200 on a part-score hand, is the sort of action that only a player who was desperate for a top might take. It's not a call one would normally contemplate, so the alternatives are:

Three Hearts
Two Hearts
Three Clubs
Two Clubs
Two Spades

The Choice

There is no intermediate bid available between the minimum bids and those that look toward game and carry the bidding to the level of Three. Thus I must first judge:

(a) Might it be a mistake to go beyond the level of Two?

(b) If we settle for one of the safer calls, is there a danger of missing game?

If the answer to both questions is affirmative, I must next consider where the balance of probability lies and other marginal factors.

To arrive at an answer to the first question we will construct some not-so-strong hands on which partner might reasonably reopen, remembering that at match points a player will contest where at rubber bridge he might not.

(1) ♠ A x ♡ A Q J x ◇ K J x x ♣ J 10 x

This wouldn't be pleasant in Three Clubs or Three Hearts.

(2) ♠ J x ♡ A K x x x ◇ A Q x ♣ Q x x

Even if the hearts are 3-2 there are five possible losers.

(3) ♠ A ♡ A K x x ◇ A 10 x x ♣ J x x x

You might make Three Clubs, but Three Hearts would be awkward. Now two hands where game would just about be possible:

(4) ♠ A x ♡ K Q 10 x x ◇ A K x ♣ Q x x

Here partner might pass a response of Two Hearts, but over Two Clubs he would go back to the major suit.

(5) ♠ J ♡ A K x x x ◇ A Q J ♣ Q J x x

Now either Four Hearts or Five Clubs would be playable. I think he would bid again over Two Hearts or Two Clubs from me.

It seems that the balance lies on the side of the weaker call. This was certainly my first impression—that if partner could not speak again over Two Clubs or Two Hearts game would seldom be worth bidding. It remains only to distinguish between the bids within the two groups.

The Stronger Bids

Three Clubs could easily be taken for a different type of hand altogether—something like K Q x x x of clubs and little else.

Two Spades has a superficial attraction because it appears to convey some strength and to leave the door open to contracts in either hearts or clubs. However, partner might think that he was being asked to bid 2NT (on a holding in spades such as Q x) or to choose between the two minor suits. Any subsequent bidding would in that case be conducted at cross-purposes.

Among the stronger bids we are left with Three Hearts, which has in fact some virtues. It makes progress toward the most likely game, and in view of the previous pass it will not be overestimated.

Two Hearts or Two Clubs?

There is not a lot to choose between these two. Hearts score better, but when partner has four cards of each suit more tricks will be made in clubs. The one is as likely to lead to game as the other, for when partner can bid Three Hearts over Two he will also be bidding Two Hearts over Two Clubs.

A subtle point that inclines me toward Two Clubs is this: If the opponents continue with Two Spades, which is not unlikely as they seem to have eight or nine between them, I am prepared to double if I have already shown my clubs. Partner will know that my defence is limited since I did not bid 1NT before. If his values include Q x x x of clubs he will remove the double. That is a more dynamic plan than bidding Two Hearts and following with Three Clubs over Two Spades, so I mark the alternatives:

Two Clubs	10
Two Hearts	8
Three Hearts	5
Two Spades	3
Three Clubs	2

Reflections on the Bidding

Many players—good ones among them—would approach this problem from an angle that I consider misleading. They would say, "I have two good tricks and partner will not expect me to have more, as I passed on the previous round. How, then, can it be right to make another weak call? I must jump to Three Clubs or Three Hearts."

One answer to that argument is that if you bid simply Two Clubs and West passes, your partner will not place you with a near-yarborough. It will register on him that the opponents have subsided after One Spade.

A more general answer is that the underlying thought—I must tell partner that I have something—is not by itself a reliable guide to the best action. There are, after all, many situations in bidding where it is right to pass equally on zero or 15 points.

The essential question to which South should direct his mind is the one posed above: "If I settle for one of the safer calls, is there much danger of our missing game?"

62. Preserving an Advantage

In a pairs event our side is vulnerable and as dealer I hold a bad hand for the system:

$$\spadesuit A K Q \quad \heartsuit K Q 8 3 \quad \diamondsuit Q J 5 3 2 \quad \clubsuit A$$

This is an awkward type of hand for players of standard systems. At Acol there are three, perhaps four, possibilities—One Diamond, Two Diamonds, Two Clubs, and 2NT. The reason why such eccentric bids as 2NT have to be considered is that a partner with fair hearts and singleton diamond may be unable to respond to a bid of One. However, the disadvantages of the other strong calls are certainly greater (e.g., Two Diamonds—2NT would be altogether unbearable for the opener), so I open **One Diamond.** West overcalls with **One Heart** and this is followed by two passes. My difficulties with this hand are far from over, the bidding having gone:

South	West	North	East
1 $\diamondsuit$	1 $\heartsuit$	Pass	Pass
?			

The Alternatives

The orthodox way to express a strong hand is to double. It might be more suitable to bid either 1NT or 2NT, and One Spade is also a possibility. To pass and let the opponents play One Heart is one way of obtaining a plus score. If we look no further, the alternatives are:

> 2NT
> 1NT
> One Spade
> Double
> Pass

The Choice

The hand totals 21 points in high cards, but its looks have not been improved by the passage of events. 13 of the points are made up of unattended honors, the second best suit has been called on the left, and the longest suit is far from establishment. To reopen with 2NT would be wildly unsound.

The Argument Against a Pass

There is a match-point argument against passing which is not obvious and needs careful stating:

Assume (*a*) that partner is so weak that a contract at the One level will be touch-and-go and that we can pick up 50 by defending against One Heart. In that case a pass will give us a fair score, but we shall make a better score by playing at a low level, as many pairs will be too high.

Assume (*b*) that partner has some values and that from 110 to 150 will be a popular score for North-South. In that case, to take an unusual view and let them play in One Heart might be a very poor result.

To put it another way, our decision to open with a quiet bid has been vindicated and we can aim now to play in the popular denomination at a low level.

Averting a Club Response

On the values held, the normal action on the second round is a take-out double. The objection to that is clear enough. It is highly probable that partner will respond Two Clubs and it will then be a guess whether you should leave it in, revert to diamonds, or hazard 2NT.

To bid 1NT or One Spade at this point reduces the likelihood of partner's bidding clubs on a poor suit. Suppose that partner holds:

♠ x x x ♡ x x x ◇ 10 x ♣ J 9 x x x

To a double he will respond Two Clubs, but 1NT or One Spade he will pass. If he takes out either of those bids into clubs, you will know that he has a good suit.

The hand would sometimes play quite well in One Spade—particularly when partner had three or four small spades and a singleton diamond. However, pursuing the argument above, I am not going to make a peculiar call that might turn out rather poorly. I am sure that if I buy the contract for 1NT we will score well on the hand, and I do not fear any response that partner may make. That is where 1NT is superior

211

to a double. The only advantage of a double is that occasionally partner may be able to respond in spades. On the other hand, when you double you more or less give up the chance of playing in 1NT. So I mark the alternatives:

$$
\begin{array}{ll}
\text{1NT} & \dots\dots\dots\dots\dots\dots\dots 10 \\
\text{Double} & \dots\dots\dots\dots\dots\dots\ 7 \\
\text{One Spade} & \dots\dots\dots\dots\dots\ 6 \\
\text{Pass} & \dots\dots\dots\dots\dots\dots\ 5 \\
\text{2NT} & \dots\dots\dots\dots\dots\dots\ 1
\end{array}
$$

Reflections on the Bidding

This discussion brought out an important principle. When in a match-pointed event you seem to have made a good decision, take care not to throw away your advantage. To give another example, say that with neither side vulnerable you are second to speak and hold:

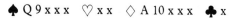

♠ Q 9 x x x   ♡ x x   ◇ A 10 x x x   ♣ x

The bidding is opened on your right with One Club. The normal action is to pass or bid One Diamond, but One Spade has some pre-emptive value and you choose that instead. The next player passes and your partner raises to Three Spades. Now don't press your luck. If you make an overtrick in Three Spades that will surely be an excellent score.

PART SEVEN

An Element of Surprise

The common factor among the hands in this final section is that someone at the table has made an irregular call or that there has been, or is about to be, a surprising development.

63. Taking the Cue

Playing in a multiple team event against opponents who are not particularly strong, I hold in fourth position:

♠ K J 8 6 3 2   ♡ Q 9   ◇ 3   ♣ J 10 9 4

We are vulnerable and after a pass by West my partner opens **One Heart.** East overcalls with **2NT** and on enquiry I learn that this is the "unusual no trump" signifying distributional strength in the minors. That prevents my natural response of One Spade and I have to think anew after the sequence:

South	West	North	East
—	Pass	1♡	2NT
?			

The Alternatives

If I decide not to be shut out, Three Spades and Three Hearts are both possible calls. I can indicate some general values by doubling 2NT, or I can pass and see how West responds. Those are the only alternatives:

Three Spades
Three Hearts
Double
Pass

The Choice

Players make this 2NT overcall on a wide variety of hands. East may be strong or he may have quite a weak 6-5 hand and be trying to obstruct us. I cannot form any reliable estimate as to whether our side is in the game zone or not.

The natural division is between a bid at the Three level and a pass or double.

No Reason to Overbid

Neither Three Spades nor Three Hearts would often be immediately disastrous, but both would be overbids and either might lead to the wrong final contract. That applies more to Three Hearts than to Three Spades. If partner raises the spades that will probably be the right suit for us, but Three Hearts could turn out to be a bad mistake if partner held something like:

$$\spadesuit \text{A Q x} \quad \heartsuit \text{A K x x x} \quad \diamondsuit \text{J x x} \quad \clubsuit \text{Q x}$$

On the other hand, Three Spades is more likely to set the opponents on the doubling trail if we have a misfit.

Often one has to take risks in face of enemy pre-emption, but I am not in a "now-or-never" situation here. If I pass or double I may have an opportunity later to show my length in spades.

A Double Creates Problems

By doubling I can tell my partner that I have some defensive strength, but this call may be difficult to follow up. For example, suppose that West takes out into Three Diamonds and partner, taking his cue from me, doubles on the strength of a trick in diamonds. It wouldn't be at all safe for me to pass the double, nor would it be sound to follow up the double with Three Spades.

I should also be in something of a dilemma if, after my double, Three Diamonds came around to me undoubled. Partner would expect me to do something, and again Three Spades, following the double of 2NT, would give the impression of a much better hand than I hold.

A Pass Seems Best

The advantage of passing now is that if I decide to defend later in Three Spades it will not sound so strong. West will probably take out into Three Diamonds, and if that comes to me, I will chance Three Spades.

It is true that if East raises the diamonds I shall be shut out of the auction, but that may not matter greatly. We shall not be missing a vulnerable game, for if the opposition can bid voluntarily to Four Diamonds, no doubt they will have some answer to Four Spades.

There seems no point in taking the risk either of bidding or doubling and I mark the alternatives:

Pass........................10
Double 5
Three Spades................ 4
Three Hearts................ 2

Reflections on the Bidding

This may not seem a very abstruse problem, but when it was set in a Dutch newspaper competition for which I acted as adjudicator there were (literally) thousands of votes for other forms of action.

The principle is easy to remember. When opponents are in a forcing sequence (or at any rate a sequence where they are likely to bid again) it is a mistake to step in either with a risky overbid or a premature double.

64. Unwanted Support

My partner at rubber bridge is an aggressive but intelligent bidder. Neither side is vulnerable and as dealer I hold:

♠ A K 4   ♡ Q 6   ◇ K 7 2   ♣ A K J 6 3

With 20 points and a useful five-card suit I have enough in theory for an opening 2NT in our system. I don't mind the moderate holding in hearts but the texture of the hand is better suited to a trump contract, so I open **One Club.** Partner responds **One Diamond.** This hand could develop in a number of ways, and for that reason I don't fancy a jump to 3NT. One Spade is a possibility, but we don't play it as forcing. I think I'll let him know at once that I've got a big hand by jumping to **Two Spades.** It should be possible to control any future developments.

Partner raises to **Three Spades.** That was liable to happen and now I have to escape from the trap I have laid for myself. The bidding so far:

South	West	North	East
1♣	Pass	1◇	Pass
2♠	Pass	3♠	Pass
?			

The Alternatives

One way of warning partner that my spades were unsubstantial would be to retreat to 3NT. Four Spades might be playable, despite the shortness of my suit. I could support my partner's diamonds now or repeat the clubs. That seems about all. Thus the alternatives are:

Four Spades
Four Diamonds
Four Clubs
3NT

I don't know much about my partner's hand. We were in a forcing situation, so he could be minimum or he could be quite strong.

Game or slam appear possible in various denominations and one bid I am not going to make is 3NT, risking ignominious defeat on a promising hand. Better to play in Four Spades with seven trumps than in 3NT with no stop in hearts!

Four Spades

Playing in spades, my hand can take the force on the third round of hearts. Four Spades will generally be playable if partner's spades are headed by the Queen, but not if he holds something like:

(1) ♠ J 9 x x   ♡ x x x   ◇ A J 10 x x   ♣ x

Now three rounds of hearts would be very awkward.

Nor is it impossible for partner to hold only three trumps. Some players will never raise on three trumps in these positions, but I don't see what else he could do on a hand like:

(2) ♠ Q J x   ♡ 10 x x   ◇ A Q x x x   ♣ x x

Four Diamonds

On the two hands I have constructed so far, Five Diamonds would be the best game chance, and Four Diamonds from me at this point would get us to that contract. With an imaginative partner the danger of supporting diamonds after this sequence is that he will think my force was based on diamond support or that I am 4-1-3-5 with a singleton heart. He may carry me too high on any of these hands:

(3) ♠ Q 10 x x   ♡ x x x   ◇ A Q J x x   ♣ x

(4) ♠ Q J 9 x   ♡ 10 x x   ◇ A Q 10 x   ♣ Q x

(5) ♠ J 10 x x   ♡ A x x   ◇ A J x x   ♣ x x

Four Clubs

This call seems to leave open the greatest number of possibilities. When he has five diamonds and his spades are not strong, partner will take the opportunity to rebid his diamonds. He will expect me, in view of the force after the One Diamond response, to have some values in the suit. If he can bid only Four Spades over Four Clubs I shall pass. Occasionally he will be able to raise the clubs—for example on:

(6) ♠ J 9 x x   ♡ x x x   ◇ A Q x x   ♣ Q x

Now the best game contract is Five Clubs.

I am just looking back to see what partner would bid over Four Clubs with the other example hands. On (1), (2), and (3) he would bid Four Diamonds; on (4) Five Clubs or Five Spades (which I would pass). On (5) he would be a bit puzzled and would probably bid Four Hearts for the moment. I would have to bid Four Spades and there we would stop.

There seems nothing much wrong with Four Clubs, and I mark the alternatives:

Four Clubs....................10
Four Spades.................. 6
Four Diamonds.............. 5
3NT 3

Reflections on the Bidding

Having made an irregular call, South must keep his head and consider carefully the effect of whatever he proposes to bid next. In their haste to escape from spades, many players would choose 3NT or Four Diamonds. The objection to these bids is worth repeating:

3NT. When there is no other clear prospect of game it is not wrong to trust that Q x in conjunction with whatever partner may hold will prove a sufficient stop; but when there should be a sound game somewhere else, the risk becomes unwise.

Four Diamonds. Misleading, because the sequence would suggest either a force based on diamond support or a powerful hand containing clubs, spades and diamonds, so with a shortage in hearts.

65. In the Picture

In a team contest our side is vulnerable and in second position I hold:

♠ 9 8 4   ♡ A 10 6 2   ◇ Q 9 2   ♣ K Q 10

East, on my right, deals and passes, I pass, and West opens with **One Diamond.** My partner **doubles** and East **redoubles.** There seems to be a lot of good hands about, the bidding having gone:

South	West	North	East
—	—	—	Pass
Pass	1◇	Double	Redouble
?			

The Alternatives

I can either pass and see what develops or make some call to reflect my values, such as a jump in hearts or no trump, or a bid of the opponent's suit. The alternatives are:

2NT
Two Hearts
Two Diamonds
Pass

The Choice

Someone at the table must be bluffing and in all probability it is West, who has opened in third position. The question that arises now is whether I should make some bid to clarify the position or pass for the moment and let the enemy find their own way out of, or into, trouble.

Possibility of a Trap Pass

At first sight it seems as though a quiet pass may be the best way to attract some indiscretion from East. If West passes, my partner, not knowing what is going on, will bid something and East may step in with some bid which I can double.

I can think of some weaknesses in that plan. First, if West has made a psychic opening he will take out the redouble—probably into Two Diamonds—to warn partner that his opening was not serious. Even if that does not happen, East, having redoubled already, will not jump to the skies. The vulnerability is not suitable to a low-level double, so on closer examination there is not much future in the trap pass as such.

The positive disadvantage of passing now is that it will be difficult afterwards to convey to partner the nature of my hand. Also, we shall have to exchange information at a higher level. I would rather look for a bid that will put him in the picture.

Two Hearts a Different Meaning

Had East passed over the double, a jump to Two Hearts would have been in order, but after the redouble it would suggest a rather different sort of hand. The presumption would be that the enemy had the balance of the cards and Two Hearts would sound like an attempt to steal the bid, or prepare for competition, on K Q J x x and not much else in the hand.

2NT Less Accurate than Two Diamonds

An immediate jump to 2NT would carry too great a risk of playing in 3NT with an inadequate holding in the enemy suit. More satisfactory is Two Diamonds, telling partner that I have a useful hand, but not necessarily forcing to game. Over Two Diamonds he will perhaps bid Two Spades; if I then introduce 2NT he will know that my holding in diamonds is sketchy. If he bids Two Hearts or 2NT I can raise. I see no disadvantage in this call and mark the alternatives:

Two Diamonds	10
2NT	7
Pass	6
Two Hearts	3

Reflections on the Bidding

What happened when this hand was actually played illustrates the danger of being too clever and keeping partner in the dark. South passed the redouble, West (who had opened on A J x x x of diamonds and a Jack) also passed, and North, who had made a minimum double on a 3-3-3-4 hand, deemed it safer to bid a low-level One Heart than to climb to 1NT or Two Clubs. The last thing he expected was a jump in hearts from his hitherto tongue-tied partner. To make it worse, South was so impressed by the need to amend his former abstinence that he jumped to Four Hearts. This failed by two tricks, while 3NT would have been easily made.

66. Contrary to System

My present opponents in a pairs contest are enterprising players, as will appear in a moment. We are vulnerable and in second position I hold:

♠ A K   ♡ Q 9 6 5 4   ◇ 10 5 3 2   ♣ K 3

East, on my right, opens **One Heart.** There's nothing I can say over that, so I pass. West responds **Two Clubs.** North passes and so does East. That, of course, is contrary to system. I have to sort out what is happening after the sequence:

South	West	North	East
—	—	—	1♡
Pass	2♣	Pass	Pass
?			

The Alternatives

The natural ways to reopen are 2NT, Two Hearts or double. Two Diamonds can hardly be right, as we do not want to play in diamonds unless partner can bid them in response to a double. On the other hand, East might be trapping and it might be unwise to reopen at all. The alternatives are:

> 2NT
> Two Hearts
> Double
> Pass

The Choice

East may be trying something new, but in general there are two classes of hand that might account for his opening the bidding and then passing over the response of Two Clubs. First, there is the out-and-out psychic, probably containing a heart suit, such as:

(1) ♠ x x   ♡ K J 10 x x   ◇ x x x   ♣ x x x

More fashionable nowadays is the semi-psychic opening on a three-card suit with about 10 or 11 points. It could be something of this sort:

(2) ♠ Q 10 x x ♡ A x x ◇ K Q 9 x ♣ x x

This sort of opening can work out well in a number of ways. It may enable East-West to steal the contract on inferior cards, it may take away the opponents' best suit, and it may set a trap when, as on the present occasion, partner's response is in the short suit. When East passes he takes a slight risk of missing game but he knows that is he putting the vulnerable opponents on the spot.

Double or 2NT Too Dangerous

If East is laying a trap of that sort I will walk right into it if I double. Knowing that his partner has responded at the Two level, East will be quick to double any take-out by my partner. Two Spades doubled could easily cost 800. To reopen with 2NT would be still more dangerous.

Pass or Two Hearts

The one bid that East will not be able to double if he has opened on a three-card suit is Two Hearts, and this I am sure is the safest way to reopen. Partner will know that the hearts are a real suit in view of my pass on the previous round.

If East has the other type of hand—just hearts—my partner will have upwards of 12 points and will be able to join in.

However, before taking action that admittedly has its risks, I must consider what sort of result a pass might bring. East, I presume, will not open the bidding at most other tables. I wouldn't open on my hand, but many will. If I reopen now, I won't be any worse off than players who have opened the bidding with One Heart. And, of course, there are dangers in passing. If we hold the balance of the cards we will not get a brilliant result by letting them play in Two Clubs.

I am going to contest with Two Hearts and I mark the alternatives:

Two Hearts 10
Pass. 6
Double 4
2NT 2

Reflections on the Bidding

Most players, I think, would double in South's position, not realizing that this was more dangerous than bidding Two Hearts.

The semi-psychic opening on a three-card suit and about 11 points is quite a clever manoeuvre. It may buy the contract, or steal the opponents' bid, or trap them into unwise defence. It is a bid that, at rubber bridge, good players often make in a part-score situation.

67. A Quick Appraisal

In a Masters Pairs event I am third to speak and hold:

♠ A J 10 5 4   ♡ 4 2   ◇ Q 10 9   ♣ 10 5 2

With neither side vulnerable, my partner opens **One Heart** and East, on my right, overcalls with **1NT.** Enquiry from his partner elicits the information that so far as he knows this is a natural bid. (Some players use an overcall of 1NT as a distributional take-out double.) The customary procedure with my scattered strength is to double the intervention, but from experience on both sides of the table I avoid this call when there is any alternative. Often I have been doubled in 1NT myself and ended with a good result. Knowing (for a good reason that will be revealed later) that my partner shares this prejudice, I overcall with **Two Spades** in preference to doubling.

West now bids **2NT,** my partner **Three Hearts,** and East **3NT.** Everyone seems to have a lot of good cards in this sequence:

South	West	North	East
—	—	1♡	1NT
2♠	2NT	3♡	3NT
?			

The Alternatives

I can remedy my omission to double 2NT by doubling 3NT! Having shown some values already, I can pass. Perhaps I should support my partner instead. The alternatives are:

Four Hearts
Double
Pass

The Choice

It is not difficult to judge what is going on. East's no trump bidding is no doubt based on long, solid clubs, and partner has more shape than points. Let's look into the matter more closely and see if we can form an opinion as to how many tricks they are likely to make at no trump and we in hearts.

Better Than a Three Heart Opening

To take our side first, the indications are that in playing values my partner has rather better than a Three Heart opening. My Two Spades over the 1NT intervention gave no promise of support for hearts, yet he has bid Three Hearts over 2NT at a moment when he was very much exposed to a double. He must hold a few cards in my suit, I should think, and the rest of his values will be in diamonds rather than clubs—if I am right in assuming that clubs are the basis of the enemy calling.

What Are Our Prospects in Hearts?

Quite good, really. My strength appears to be well placed. My doubleton heart represents adequate support in this sequence. East's persistence to 3NT over Three Hearts suggests a single stop only, for with a double stop he might have preferred to double.

Can We Beat 3NT?

We might not. At any rate, I can picture them winning the first heart and running off six or seven clubs. If East has the Ace of diamonds as well, they may make nine tricks before we get started. Looking at it another way, there is nothing in my hand to suggest that East will be disappointed in his evident expectation to go very close to 3NT.

The Match-point Angle

If I double 3NT and we beat it by one trick, that may not be a good result, for I dare say that some pairs our way will be making 140 or 170 in a part score. I can pass 3NT to my partner but I don't suppose he will be able to do any more. It's for me to make the decision. I am going to bid Four Hearts and I mark the alternatives:

$$
\begin{array}{ll}
\text{Four Hearts} \dots\dots\dots\dots\dots\dots & 10 \\
\text{Pass} \dots\dots\dots\dots\dots\dots\dots\dots & 5 \\
\text{Double} \dots\dots\dots\dots\dots\dots\dots & 3 \\
\end{array}
$$

Reflections on the Bidding

This situation arose in the Masters Pairs of 1962 in London, and at my table I actually held the North, not the South, cards. My partner, Boris Schapiro, bid Four Hearts over 3NT without seeming to give the matter a moment's consideration. It turned out well, for the heart hand was:

♠ 9 8 3　♡ K Q 10 8 7 6 3　◇ K J 6　♣ —

East could have made 3NT, and while there was a difficult defence that would have beaten Four Hearts doubled, in practice we made it.

Not everyone can be so quick on the uptake as to make this Four Heart bid in a flash, but when the bidding around the table doesn't seem to "add up," that is the time to stop and work out what is going on.

68. Reprieve

Playing rubber bridge in a tough school I deal myself the following assortment with both sides vulnerable:

♠ J 7 5 3 2   ♡ 4   ◇ 8 6 5 3   ♣ 7 4 2

I pass and West, on my left, opens **2NT**. My natural assumption that the rubber has gone west is temporarily suspended when partner overcalls 2NT with **3NT**. East passes with a straight face and I have to consider my action after this sequence:

South	West	North	East
Pass	2NT	3NT	Pass
?			

The Alternatives

Whatever interpretation is placed on this strange affair, a pass must come into consideration. Perhaps, however, this is the unusual no trump, asking for my better minor suit, or perhaps, on the analogy of 2NT over 1NT, my partner has an unspecified two-suiter. As this might consist of hearts and clubs, my best response in this case would be Four Clubs. I can't believe that he wants to hear Four Spades from me, so the alternatives are:

Four Diamonds
Four Clubs
Pass

The Choice

What shall I do? Offer him a hearing aid? Ask (unethically) for a review of the bidding?

Is it possible that partner thinks it is I who opened 2NT and that he is raising me to Three? That would leave East with enough points to double. I had better assume that West and North have all the cards and consider what partner means by his 3NT.

Can He Have a Two-suiter?

An overcall of 2NT over an opponent's 1NT is conventionally a force denoting a big two-suiter. If partner is on the same track here his hand will look something like:

$$(1) \spadesuit — \quad \heartsuit K Q 10 x x x \quad \diamondsuit x \quad \clubsuit A Q J x x x$$

This seems a more probable construction than that he has bid an unusual no trump on the strength of minor suits. That would leave too many hearts missing, and we would have heard from East.

But with the hand above, would he use this ambiguous method? I think he would bid a simple Three Hearts, expecting to have an opportunity to show the clubs later if that seemed advisable.

Can He Have a Genuine Bid?

Not an all-round hand, for then he would double, and in any event he could not have enough points unless West had made an extraordinary vulnerable psychic. But he could have a hand on which he might judge 3NT to be a good prospect, something like:

$$(2) \spadesuit x x \quad \heartsuit A K Q 10 x x x \quad \diamondsuit K x \quad \clubsuit A J$$
Or:
$$(3) \spadesuit A \quad \heartsuit A K Q 10 x x x \quad \diamondsuit Q x x \quad \clubsuit K x$$

These hands add up to 17 and 18 points respectively, so there would just be enough left for West to have a genuine bid (20 to 22 being the standard in our school).

What sort of a bid would 3NT be on either of these hands? Rather a clever trick, really. He could double 2NT but would not expect the double to be left in. He could pass and hope for an easy 400 or so. But he might be more ambitious, expecting to be doubled in 3NT and to make it. Certainly 3NT represents a better chance than Four Hearts.

If partner has made this imaginative call he will not thank me for removing it. I mark the alternatives:

$$\begin{array}{ll} \text{Pass} & 10 \\ \text{Four Clubs} & 4 \\ \text{Four Diamonds} & 1 \end{array}$$

Reflections on the Bidding

This was a somewhat fanciful situation, but opportunities do occur for the type of bid attributed to North. With hand (3) he could make the same overcall over an opening 1NT or over One Diamond or One Club. Such bids are usually based on a minor suit and so are psychologically more effective when based on a major.

69. Escape Route

My partner in a rubber bridge game is normally a sensible bidder. We are vulnerable when I deal and pick up:

♠ A J 8   ♡ J 5 2   ◇ A Q 8 5 3   ♣ Q 7

I open **One Diamond** and he responds **One Heart.** As I have tenaces in three suits I rebid **1NT** rather than support the hearts or (grisly notion) repeat the diamonds. Partner takes out into **Two Clubs.** He could still be quite weak, so I just give preference to **Two Hearts.** Now he bids **Three Clubs.** That is a little puzzling, the bidding having gone:

South	West	North	East
1◇	Pass	1♡	Pass
1NT	Pass	2♣	Pass
2♡	Pass	3♣	Pass
?			

The Alternatives

If I assume that partner is looking for game I can sign off in Three Hearts; bid the game either in hearts or no trump; or try the effect of Three Spades, which he will know is not a genuine suit. On the other hand, if Three Clubs is intended to signify that he prefers to play there rather than in Two Hearts, a pass is indicated. One or two other bids, such as Three Diamonds or Four Clubs, are conceivable, but certainly not the best, so we will list the alternatives as:

Four Hearts
Three Hearts
3NT
Three Spades
Pass

The Choice

Now what is this bid of Three Clubs supposed to be? Is this rebid of his second suit, when I have supported his first suit, an invitation to game on a hand containing two five-card suits? Then his hand will be something like this:

(1) ♠ x x ♡ K Q x x x ◇ x ♣ K J 10 x x

On that assumption my bid would obviously be Four Hearts. 3NT would be a mistake, and Three Spades would be pointless.

But if my partner had wanted to make a try for game over Two Hearts, I think he would have found a less ambiguous call, such as Three Hearts. The other possibility is that he has much longer clubs than hearts and that he responded One Heart because he was not strong enough to respond at the level of Two. An example would be:

(2) ♠ x x x ♡ K Q x x ◇ — ♣ J 10 x x x x

Such hands play vilely in Two Hearts with only three trumps opposite. Of the two interpretations I think that the second is more likely. It is also the safer assumption to follow, for if I am wrong then at worst we will play a part-score contract instead of a game which will not necessarily be a lay-down. If I miscalculated in the other direction, bidding Four Hearts opposite hand (2), we might run into an 800 penalty. In that sense Three Spades, leaving room for partner to bid Four Clubs, is less dangerous than Four Hearts, and I mark the alternatives:

Pass........................10
Three Spades................ 5
Three Hearts................ 4
3NT 4
Four Hearts................. 2

233

Reflections on the Bidding

The marking is somewhat artificial because the situation is really this: If Three Clubs is to be read as a try for game, the answer is Four Hearts. If Three Clubs is an attempt to wriggle out of hearts, the answer is Pass.

During the discussion, we treated this as a practical problem and adopted the safer solution. I have no doubt that it is also the right theoretical solution. That is to say, the most useful employment of Three Clubs in the sequence under review is as an escape from hearts.

70. Pleasant Dreams

Most players have their day-dreams, and in one such dream I deal myself at rubber bridge:

♠ —　♡ —　◇ —　♣ A K Q J 10 9 8 7 6 5 4 3 2

My side is vulnerable and the problem is my opening call. To preserve the harmonies I set out the bidding diagram in the usual style:

South	West	North	East
?			

The Alternatives

These will occupy more space than the bidding. Seven Clubs cannot be excluded, nor Six Clubs, nor . . . A case could be made for any number of clubs and some would account it clever to pass. We will examine them all:

> Seven Clubs
> Six Clubs
> Five Clubs
> Four Clubs
> Three Clubs
> Two Clubs (conventional)
> One Club
> Pass

The Choice

Let us be clear about the objectives: To play the hand in Seven Clubs doubled would be agreeable, but the first objective is to play the hand in clubs, period. Even Five Clubs undoubled with 150 honors is sweeter than a 300 or 500 penalty against opponents sacrificing at the level of Seven.

The possible openings fall into three groups: the big bids (Seven Clubs, Six Clubs, and Two Clubs); the quiet calls (One Club and pass); and the deceptive pre-empts (Three Clubs, Four Clubs, and Five Clubs). Let us take these three groups in turn.

The Big Bids

Seven Clubs from hand, vulnerable! They might believe it or they might not, but a defender with a long suit would surely follow the safer course of sacrificing.

Six Clubs? A better chance, certainly. If they don't overcall we make a good score, and if they do they may still let me play at the range of Seven.

The idea of bidding a conventional Two Clubs would be to put up a pretence in the later auction that partner's response had improved the hand. This plan might work out well if partner took vigorous action but would fall flat if he had little to say. Meanwhile, the opponents would have a chance to get together and at a high level would be the more disposed to sacrifice.

The Quiet Calls

If I pass to begin with and then go higher and higher in clubs, vulnerable, will anyone be deceived? Hardly! Opening One Club I shall again be dependent on vigorous action from my partner. If most of the bidding is done by the opponents, they will realize that there is something very strange in the air when I go on bidding and bidding.

The Pseudo Pre-empts

Three Clubs is open to the same objection as the calls in the last group. No one will credit a player who opens Three Clubs and then tries to play in Seven Clubs . . .

With the higher pre-empts I stand a better chance. It is not in-conceivable that a player who opened Four Clubs should contest at a higher level. That is even truer of a player who opens Five Clubs and may have ten or eleven tricks in his own hand, plus honors. After that it would not sound suspicious to follow with Six and even Seven Clubs. There is, however, the disadvantage that if the outstanding strength at the table is equally divided no one may overcall at this level. In this respect there is a big difference between Four Clubs and Five Clubs.

Summing Up

It is not easy to decide between the bids I fancy—Four Clubs, Five Clubs, and Six Clubs. Six Clubs will produce a good score if not overcalled, and there will be nothing suspicious in continuing to Seven; but opponents may persist in their sacrifice. Five Clubs will work well so long as someone bids over it. Bidding Four Clubs, I think that, at worst, I will be able to play in Five or Six Clubs doubled. The disadvantage of the lower opening bids is that one may be left with the task of making the running and any deliberate jump will be too obvious a sign of strength. On the understanding that after opening Four Clubs or Five Clubs I intend to advance only by minimum stages, I mark the alternatives:

> Four Clubs 10
> Five Clubs 9
> Six Clubs 7
> Two Clubs 6
> One Club 5
> Three Clubs 4
> Seven Clubs 3
> Pass 3

Reflections on the Bidding

This little fantasy is not without serious meaning. The point I want to bring out is that when you have an extreme freak and have reason to fear that you may be overcalled at a high level, you must not be impatient, and you must be sure that your tactical underbidding has some verisimilitude about it. To give a more practical example, you hold:

$$\spadesuit — \quad \heartsuit — \quad \diamondsuit A J 9 8 7 6 4 2 \quad \clubsuit K Q 8 6 4$$

The bidding begins:

South	West	North	East
—	1♠	2♣	2♡
?			

Now it is not clever to pass or attempt some psychic manoeuvre. If you do that, the opponents will realize in time that you were bluffing on a giant. Your objective is to be allowed to play in Six or Seven Clubs, apparently sacrificing. Begin, then, with the sort of bid you might make on a weaker hand. Five Clubs would be a good choice.

71. Auxiliary Guard

My partner in a team-of-four match is a good player, but we have not played a lot together. With both sides vulnerable, I hold in third position:

♠ 9 7 6 3   ♡ A J 10 5 3   ◇ A K 10 8   ♣ —

Partner opens **One Club,** and the next player passes. I respond **One Heart,** and he rebids **1NT.** Some players treat a rebid of 1NT as fairly strong, but we have no understanding to that effect, and I take him for a moderate balanced hand of about 13 to 15 points. Even so, I have enough for game. Since a simple change of suit over 1NT would not be forcing, I jump to **Three Diamonds.** I intend to raise Three Hearts to Four, or to pass 3NT. But partner has another idea—**Three Spades.** That makes an unusual sequence:

South	West	North	East
—	—	1♣	Pass
1♡	Pass	1NT	Pass
3◇	Pass	3♠	Pass
?			

The Alternatives

This bid of Three Spades is open to a number of possible interpretations, such as:

(a) North has a fair spade suit which he might have shown on the second round.

(b) He is ready to play in 3NT if I have an auxiliary stop, or at any rate some length, in spades.

(c) He was much encouraged by the force in diamonds and is making an advance cue-bid, showing the Ace of spades before supporting diamonds.

If I read him for a spade suit I would raise to Four Spades, and if I thought he was asking for 3NT I would bid that. If I were sure that Three Spades was an advance cue-bid confirming diamonds, my best bid for the moment would be a return cue-bid of Four Clubs, taking this opportunity to show the void. The alternatives are therefore:

Four Spades
Four Clubs
3NT

If I accepted the advance cue-bid theory, then Four Hearts, showing the Ace, or a Culbertson 4NT, showing two Aces and the King of a bid suit, would also be possible bids. But as the problem is mainly one of interpretation, we will stay with Four Clubs.

The Choice

Let us examine the three possibilities above. First, has North a genuine spade suit which he is prepared for me to raise? Suppose he held:

(1) ♠ A J 10 x ♡ K x ◇ Q x x ♣ K x x x

After One Club—One Heart he might suppress the spade suit for tactical reasons, hoping for a spade lead against no trump. But having started on that line, would he bid Three Spades over Three Diamonds, and, if so, with what object? He would scarcely think the suit worth showing, as a suit, after I had bid two other suits. He would either persist with his original plan and bid 3NT, or he might give false preference to hearts.

It is more likely that he wants to show strength in spades for a different reason, holding:

(2) ♠ A K 10 ♡ x x ◇ Q x x ♣ A x x x x

Now, he might want to convey the message, "If you are worried about spades for 3NT, I hold them well. If you have other plans, this will tell you that I have more honor strength in spades than clubs."

He wouldn't expect me to be able to raise to Four Spades at this late date, however, and that answers the supposition that his Three Spades might be a genuine suit.

Can He Be Asking for 3NT?

The second theory was that he might be suggesting 3NT if I could help in spades. For example, he might hold:

(3) ♠ A 10 x   ♡ x x   ◇ Q J x   ♣ A Q 10 x x°

He would not expect to make 3NT if I had a singleton spade.
Another possibility of the same sort:

(4) ♠ Q 10 x   ♡ Q x   ◇ J x x   ♣ A K J x x

With so uncertain a guard in the unbid suit he would hesitate to bid 3NT himself, but at the same time would not want to by-pass that contract in case I held J x or something of that kind. Then there might be too many top losers in a suit contract.

Both these constructions are possible. 3NT certainly cannot be ruled out.

Could Three Spades Be an Advance Cue-bid, Confirming Diamonds?

Possibly. It would be a hand of this type:

(5) ♠ A x   ♡ K x   ◇ Q J x x   ♣ K J x x x

Now Three Diamonds would excite him and Three Spades, to be followed by support for diamonds, would be a sound manoeuvre. With this fit there would be a good play for Six Diamonds.

However, if that is his intention, he will clarify by bidding Four Diamonds over 3NT. Thus, an imaginative Four Clubs on my part at this stage is unnecessary and could easily be misread.

The more I look at it the more it seems that 3NT is most likely what he wants to hear and also will not be fatal if he has other plans. Even if he has a spade suit we may well make 3NT, and if he is heading for a slam in diamonds, that is not ruled out by my bidding 3NT. So I mark the alternatives:

$$3NT \dots\dots\dots\dots\dots\dots\dots 10$$
$$\text{Four Spades} \dots\dots\dots\dots\dots\dots 3$$
$$\text{Four Clubs} \dots\dots\dots\dots\dots\dots 3$$

When partner has made a somewhat ambiguous bid, as certainly North did here, it is wise to consider not only, "What does he mean?" but also "What bid can I make that will allow for more than one possibility?" It is on these grounds that 3NT is clearly right on this hand. Even if based on a misunderstanding of partner's holding, it will still not lead to a calamity, as might any of the other bids.

Did you note the inference that led us to conclude that partner had not bid spades as a genuine suit? We reflected that after this sequence he would not expect South to be able to support, so would not bid the suit with that idea in mind.

Glance again at hands (3) and (4) and the suggested bid of Three Spades. This is a good example of modern tactics in such a situation. If North held the unbid suit strongly enough for 3NT he would make that bid himself. When instead he calls the suit the message is, "If you can contribute a little support in this quarter then we should be in 3NT."

72. Do We Like It?

In a rubber bridge game of high standard the opponents are vulnerable, we are not. East, on my right, opens **One Heart** and my hand is:

♠ J 10 4 2   ♡ 9 8 4 2   ◇ K Q 9   ♣ 8 4

I pass, West responds **One Spade,** and East rebids **Two Hearts.** This is passed to my partner, who **doubles.** When East passes, my first task is to decipher the meaning of the double after the sequence:

South	West	North	East
—	—	—	1♡
Pass	1♠	Pass	2♡
Pass	Pass	Double	Pass
?			

The Alternatives

North's double could be interpreted in three ways: as a penalty double, which I would happily pass; as a request for one of the unbid suits, to which I would have to respond with Three Diamonds; or as a hand with all-round strength apart from hearts, in which case Two Spades would be the most economical response. I can't imagine 2NT being a good bid in any circumstance, so the alternatives are:

Three Diamonds
Two Spades
Pass

The Choice

Partner would not take a foolish risk at this vulnerability, so I can take it that he was strong enough to enter the bidding on the first round, but was prevented by some tactical consideration. With a strong minor two-suiter he could have come in over One Spade, and with a distributional two-suiter the bid he would choose now is 2NT, not Double. Thus I am sure it would not be right for me to bid a three-card minor suit.

Can the Double Be for Penalties?

Inconceivable, really. To double for penalties, sitting under the heart bidder, he would need a very strong trump holding. East, who has bid hearts twice, must hold five at least, probably six, and I hold four, so there are not many left for partner. He may have a generally defensive hand on which he would be happy to hear me pass the double if I had tricks in hearts, but he himself must be short of hearts.

Has Partner Length in Spades?

That is the natural conclusion from his bidding up to now. It would explain why he did not enter on the previous round. Holding strength in the suit bid on his right, he was waiting to see how the bidding would develop.

Once that inference has been drawn, it becomes apparent that my best bid is Two Spades. That will work well if partner holds something of this sort:

$$\spadesuit A Q 9 x \quad \heartsuit x \quad \diamondsuit A 10 x \quad \clubsuit Q 10 x x x$$

Such an example is sufficient to point the folly of passing or bidding Three Diamonds. The bid I dismissed earlier, 2NT, would in fact be less destructive than passing the double, so we should perhaps give it a place in the marking:

Two Spades	10
Three Diamonds	4
(2NT	3)
Pass	1

Reflections on the Bidding

When a player fails to overcall on the first round of bidding and reopens later in circumstances that suggest he must hold a good hand, it can generally be assumed that he is strong in the first suit bid on his right.

This problem was set in a bidding competition promoted for its readers by a Belgian newspaper. The panel of experts who answered the questions all interpreted North's double in the sense I have described, and so found the same answer, Two Spades. Of 5,842 readers, however, no fewer than 4,486 were prepared to pass the double of Two Hearts. One can only assume that they forgot to ask, "Why did North not bid on the previous round?" and "Can he possibly have the trump strength to make a penalty double at the range of Two?"

73. Time for Discretion

In a team event I am fourth to speak and hold:

♠ A 6 3   ♡ J 9 7 4 2   ◇ 10 6   ♣ K 8 5

Neither side is vulnerable and West, on my left, opens **Three Diamonds.** My partner overcalls with **Four Diamonds,** and while I am wondering how to deal with that, East bids **Five Diamonds.** I enter the auction for the first time at the range of Five:

South	West	North	East
—	3◇	4◇	5◇
?			

The Alternatives

In our system, the normal bid for a take-out over Three of a minor suit is a double. The overcall in the opponent's suit conventionally denotes a powerful two-suiter. I could pass now to enable my partner to declare himself, I could attempt to express my general values with a double or 5NT, or I could bid Five Hearts freely. As my Ace of spades and King of clubs are good cards to hold after this sequence, I could also bid Six Diamonds to extract a choice from my partner, or Six Hearts. That makes quite a few alternatives:

> Six Hearts
> Five Hearts
> Six Diamonds
> 5NT
> Double
> Pass

In view of my length in hearts, the most likely construction of my partner's hand is a two-suiter made up of spades and clubs. He would overcall Three Diamonds with Four Diamonds on a hand of this type:

(1) ♠ K Q 10 x x   ♡ A x   ◊ —   ♣ A Q 10 x x x

He would plan to bid Four Spades if I responded with Four Hearts. He would expect me then to read him for a spade-club two-suiter and to amend to Five Clubs if I had a singleton spade and three clubs.

I feel that there should be a playable slam somewhere, and my first objective is to discover the nature of his presumed two-suiter. Let us examine the possible calls in turn.

Pass

I could pass Five Diamonds to see what he would call. Then if he bid Five Hearts or Five Spades I could raise to Six. If he doubled I could transfer to 5NT, perhaps, and then he would bid one of his suits. This seems a fair solution, but I can think of two small disadvantages. One is that if he had stretched a little to make the overcall of Four Diamonds he might be unable to bid over Five Diamonds. The other drawback is that he would not realize I was so strong, and we would have little chance to reach a possible grand slam. If I pass, I am temporarily deceiving him.

Double

Sometimes a double is the only way to indicate some general values, but here it would be misleading. Partner might conclude that I was lacking top cards and was warning him not to persist with his two-suiter.

Five Hearts

I can imagine circumstances in which this bid would put a considerable strain on partner. Suppose that he had a fair holding in hearts, such as A 10 or K Q alone. He might reflect that since he had indicated a two-suiter, I would not voluntarily introduce a suit of my own at this level unless it were strong. So he might pass and we would play in the wrong suit. Apart from this possibility, the bid would give no picture of my two key cards in the black suits.

Six Hearts

This would be an even worse mistake. Partner would think that my hearts needed little or no support and might leave me in with a singleton.

Six Diamonds

This would convey my strength but has the disadvantage of excluding Six Clubs. Partner might hold:

(2) ♠ K 9 x x x   ♡ A K   ◇ —   ♣ A Q J 9 x x

Now Six Spades would be at the mercy of the trump break, while Six Clubs would have to be very unlucky to fail.

5NT

Partner will not take this as a natural bid, for if I had a trick in diamonds I would double Five Diamonds. He will understand it as a general slam try telling him that I can play at the level of Six in whatever suit he chooses. This seems clearly best, and I mark the alternatives:

5NT	10
Pass	6
Six Diamonds	5
Double	4
Five Hearts	3
Six Hearts	1

Reflections on the Bidding

The overcall in an opponent's suit at this level to denote a two-suiter is a useful weapon, but it has to be used with discretion. For example, with a two-suiter consisting of spades and hearts it is dangerous to bid Four Diamonds over Three Diamonds because partner may have no alternative but to respond with Five Clubs. For that reason (though this was not mentioned in the discussion above), there was a fair inference for South that his partner's hand contained clubs, and a jump to Six Clubs would actually be more intelligent than many of the calls listed.

The responder's duty is to bear in mind that his partner has a two-suited, not a three-suited, hand. He must avoid any call such as Six Hearts in the present sequence that may cut right across partner's intentions.

74. The Joker

At rubber bridge my opponents are good players and one of them is something of a jester, as events will show. My partner is also a competent player. We are vulnerable and in second position I hold:

♠ A J 9 4　♡ 5　♢ K 10 6　♣ A K Q J 9

East, on my right, opens **1NT.** They are playing, in theory, a weak no trump of 13 to 15 points not vulnerable. I **double,** West passes, and so does my partner. The opener now removes himself to—**Four Hearts!** When I recover from the shock, what do I do after the sequence:

South	West	North	East
—	—	—	1NT
Double	Pass	Pass	4♡
?			

The Alternatives

I can bid one of my suits, either spades or clubs. 4NT would be an exaggeration and might be misunderstood. I can double Four Hearts or I can pass and see what my partner will do. The alternatives are:

Five Clubs
Four Spades
Double
Pass

The Choice

East, I assume, has a hand on which he could have opened with a pre-emptive Four Hearts. It must be a strong hand of that type, because after the double of his psychic 1NT he must realize that he is not going to play undoubled. I should imagine that he has about eight or nine tricks in his own hand.

Not a lot can be inferred from my partner's pass of 1NT doubled except that he is fairly balanced. Even if quite weak he may prefer defending against 1NT to bidding a poor suit at the Two level.

We can probably defeat Four Hearts, but I doubt whether we can beat it enough to compensate for a vulnerable game. East understands the mathematics of rubber bridge and would not walk into a 500 penalty. 300, less 100 honors, is closer to the mark.

The only conclusion we have reached so far is that a game will be worth much more to us than any penalty we are likely to collect. If I had to choose between the suits I would bid Five Clubs rather than Four Spades, but the fact that partner has passed the double of 1NT by no means establishes that we can make eleven tricks in clubs. He need be no better than:

(1) ♠ Q x x ♡ x x x ◇ Q x x x ♣ x x x

Five Clubs won't go like a bomb with this hand opposite, especially if the trumps are 4-1.

Double or Pass?

Since we are not sure of a game, it may seem at first sight as though we should accept what we can from a double. But if I pass, what will partner do? I think he will take it that a hand good enough to double 1NT is also good enough to double Four Hearts. In other words, he will treat my pass as forcing. On a moderate balanced hand he will double, but if he has a fair suit he will bid it, realizing that is what I am asking him to do.

(2) ♠ Q x ♡ x x x ◇ A J 9 x x ♣ x x x

With this hand he will bid Five Diamonds. He will bid Four Spades with any five-card suit, and also on:

(3) ♠ K Q x x ♡ x x x ◇ Q J x x ♣ x x

My pass at this point will be the same in effect as a take-out double of Four Hearts. That is just the message I want to convey, and I mark the alternatives:

Pass........................10
Double 5
Five Clubs 4
Four Spades................ 3

251

Reflections on the Bidding

I came into my club one evening to find a group at the bar hotly disputing this situation, which had arisen during the afternoon game. "South must double," said one. "Five Clubs," said another, and "Four Spades," insisted a third, showing clever hindsight, for North's actual hand was:

♠ Q 10 x x　♡ x x　♢ A x x x　♣ 10 x x

Whether on this hand North would have bid Four Spades after a pass by South is doubtful, I admit. Probably he would double.

The principle that emerges from this example is that when a player has already expressed his values he should not be in a hurry to bid in front of his partner. A forcing pass is one of the most eloquent calls in the game.

75. He's Trying, Too

My partner in a pairs event is an imaginative but not a wild bidder. The opponents are vulnerable and in fourth position I hold:

♠ Q 9 6 3 ♡ Q 10 ◇ A J 10 5 2 ♣ Q 9

West, the dealer on my left, opens **One Heart,** North passes, and East raises to **Two Hearts.** I pass, West bids **Four Hearts,** and now partner suddenly enters with a **double.** East passes and I have to disentangle the bidding which up to now has been:

South	West	North	East
—	1♡	Pass	2♡
Pass	4♡	Double	Pass
?			

The Alternatives

When considered in conjunction with my hand, the bidding is mysterious, but I could take the view that no one had asked me to bid. If the double seemed so unlikely as to demand a rescue, I could take out either into Four Spades or Five Diamonds. The alternatives are:

Five Diamonds
Four Spades
Pass

The Choice

On the surface, partner's double is for penalties, but if East-West, who are vulnerable, are bidding normally, it is impossible for partner to have any sort of penalty double. The only solution that makes any sense is that he lacked the strength for a take-out double on the first round but is strong enough in distribution to believe that we can save profitably at the Five level. He must be 5-4-4-0, with a hand of this sort:

(1) ♠ K 10 x x ♡ — ♢ K 9 x x ♣ 10 8 x x x

(2) ♠ J x x x x ♡ — ♢ Q 9 x x ♣ A x x x

He will be prepared for me to pass if I have a couple of trump tricks and no suit, but otherwise he will expect me to rescue.

Four Spades or Five Diamonds?

The only question that remains is whether I should take out into Four Spades or Five Diamonds. If the result at most tables is going to be 620 or 650 to East-West, it won't make much difference whether we go down three, or one, or even make our contract! What we must avoid is a 700 loss, which would be fatal. That might happen in Four Spades if partner held hand (1) and the spades and diamonds both broke badly. Five Diamonds, with nine trumps, would almost certainly be proof against 700. However, I don't have to decide that now. I can bid Four Spades for the moment and judge later whether to retreat to Five Diamonds. I mark the alternatives:

Four Spades.................10
Five Diamonds 8
Pass....................... 2

Reflections on the Bidding

This situation occurred in actual play. North held the second of the two hands quoted above, so that it would have paid to sacrifice in either spades or diamonds.

When the problem was later submitted to a panel of experts, more than half gave a pass as their answer. It is true that the solution is not readily apparent but, as the editor of the feature remarked, truthfully if not elegantly, "Because a problem may seem bizarre at first glance is no reason not to think it through imaginatively."

A CATALOGUE OF SELECTED DOVER BOOKS
IN ALL FIELDS OF INTEREST

A CATALOGUE OF SELECTED DOVER BOOKS
IN ALL FIELDS OF INTEREST

AMERICA'S OLD MASTERS, James T. Flexner. Four men emerged unexpectedly from provincial 18th century America to leadership in European art: Benjamin West, J. S. Copley, C. R. Peale, Gilbert Stuart. Brilliant coverage of lives and contributions. Revised, 1967 edition. 69 plates. 365pp. of text.

21806-6 Paperbound $3.00

FIRST FLOWERS OF OUR WILDERNESS: AMERICAN PAINTING, THE COLONIAL PERIOD, James T. Flexner. Painters, and regional painting traditions from earliest Colonial times up to the emergence of Copley, West and Peale Sr., Foster, Gustavus Hesselius, Feke, John Smibert and many anonymous painters in the primitive manner. Engaging presentation, with 162 illustrations. xxii + 368pp.

22180-6 Paperbound $3.50

THE LIGHT OF DISTANT SKIES: AMERICAN PAINTING, 1760-1835, James T. Flexner. The great generation of early American painters goes to Europe to learn and to teach: West, Copley, Gilbert Stuart and others. Allston, Trumbull, Morse; also contemporary American painters—primitives, derivatives, academics—who remained in America. 102 illustrations. xiii + 306pp. 22179-2 Paperbound $3.50

A HISTORY OF THE RISE AND PROGRESS OF THE ARTS OF DESIGN IN THE UNITED STATES, William Dunlap. Much the richest mine of information on early American painters, sculptors, architects, engravers, miniaturists, etc. The only source of information for scores of artists, the major primary source for many others. Unabridged reprint of rare original 1834 edition, with new introduction by James T. Flexner, and 394 new illustrations. Edited by Rita Weiss. 6⅝ x 9⅝.

21695-0, 21696-9, 21697-7 Three volumes, Paperbound $13.50

EPOCHS OF CHINESE AND JAPANESE ART, Ernest F. Fenollosa. From primitive Chinese art to the 20th century, thorough history, explanation of every important art period and form, including Japanese woodcuts; main stress on China and Japan, but Tibet, Korea also included. Still unexcelled for its detailed, rich coverage of cultural background, aesthetic elements, diffusion studies, particularly of the historical period. 2nd, 1913 edition. 242 illustrations. lii + 439pp. of text.

20364-6, 20365-4 Two volumes, Paperbound $6.00

THE GENTLE ART OF MAKING ENEMIES, James A. M. Whistler. Greatest wit of his day deflates Oscar Wilde, Ruskin, Swinburne; strikes back at inane critics, exhibitions, art journalism; aesthetics of impressionist revolution in most striking form. Highly readable classic by great painter. Reproduction of edition designed by Whistler. Introduction by Alfred Werner. xxxvi + 334pp.

21875-9 Paperbound $2.50

VISUAL ILLUSIONS: THEIR CAUSES, CHARACTERISTICS, AND APPLICATIONS, Matthew Luckiesh. Thorough description and discussion of optical illusion, geometric and perspective, particularly; size and shape distortions, illusions of color, of motion; natural illusions; use of illusion in art and magic, industry, etc. Most useful today with op art, also for classical art. Scores of effects illustrated. Introduction by William H. Ittleson. 100 illustrations. xxi + 252pp.

21530-X Paperbound $2.00

A HANDBOOK OF ANATOMY FOR ART STUDENTS, Arthur Thomson. Thorough, virtually exhaustive coverage of skeletal structure, musculature, etc. Full text, supplemented by anatomical diagrams and drawings and by photographs of undraped figures. Unique in its comparison of male and female forms, pointing out differences of contour, texture, form. 211 figures, 40 drawings, 86 photographs. xx + 459pp. 5⅜ x 8⅜.

21163-0 Paperbound $3.50

150 MASTERPIECES OF DRAWING, Selected by Anthony Toney. Full page reproductions of drawings from the early 16th to the end of the 18th century, all beautifully reproduced: Rembrandt, Michelangelo, Dürer, Fragonard, Urs, Graf, Wouwerman, many others. First-rate browsing book, model book for artists. xviii + 150pp. 8⅜ x 11¼.

21032-4 Paperbound $2.50

THE LATER WORK OF AUBREY BEARDSLEY, Aubrey Beardsley. Exotic, erotic, ironic masterpieces in full maturity: Comedy Ballet, Venus and Tannhauser, Pierrot, Lysistrata, Rape of the Lock, Savoy material, Ali Baba, Volpone, etc. This material revolutionized the art world, and is still powerful, fresh, brilliant. With *The Early Work,* all Beardsley's finest work. 174 plates, 2 in color. xiv + 176pp. 8⅛ x 11.

21817-1 Paperbound $3.00

DRAWINGS OF REMBRANDT, Rembrandt van Rijn. Complete reproduction of fabulously rare edition by Lippmann and Hofstede de Groot, completely reedited, updated, improved by Prof. Seymour Slive, Fogg Museum. Portraits, Biblical sketches, landscapes, Oriental types, nudes, episodes from classical mythology—All Rembrandt's fertile genius. Also selection of drawings by his pupils and followers. "Stunning volumes," *Saturday Review.* 550 illustrations. lxxviii + 552pp. 9⅛ x 12¼.

21485-0, 21486-9 Two volumes, Paperbound $10.00

THE DISASTERS OF WAR, Francisco Goya. One of the masterpieces of Western civilization—83 etchings that record Goya's shattering, bitter reaction to the Napoleonic war that swept through Spain after the insurrection of 1808 and to war in general. Reprint of the first edition, with three additional plates from Boston's Museum of Fine Arts. All plates facsimile size. Introduction by Philip Hofer, Fogg Museum. v + 97pp. 9⅜ x 8¼.

21872-4 Paperbound $2.00

GRAPHIC WORKS OF ODILON REDON. Largest collection of Redon's graphic works ever assembled: 172 lithographs, 28 etchings and engravings, 9 drawings. These include some of his most famous works. All the plates from *Odilon Redon: oeuvre graphique complet,* plus additional plates. New introduction and caption translations by Alfred Werner. 209 illustrations. xxvii + 209pp. 9⅛ x 12¼.

21966-8 Paperbound $4.00

DESIGN BY ACCIDENT; A BOOK OF "ACCIDENTAL EFFECTS" FOR ARTISTS AND DESIGNERS, James F. O'Brien. Create your own unique, striking, imaginative effects by "controlled accident" interaction of materials: paints and lacquers, oil and water based paints, splatter, crackling materials, shatter, similar items. Everything you do will be different; first book on this limitless art, so useful to both fine artist and commercial artist. Full instructions. 192 plates showing "accidents," 8 in color. viii + 215pp. 8⅜ x 11¼.   21942-9 Paperbound $3.50

THE BOOK OF SIGNS, Rudolf Koch. Famed German type designer draws 493 beautiful symbols: religious, mystical, alchemical, imperial, property marks, runes, etc. Remarkable fusion of traditional and modern. Good for suggestions of timelessness, smartness, modernity. Text. vi + 104pp. 6⅛ x 9¼.
                                        20162-7 Paperbound $1.25

HISTORY OF INDIAN AND INDONESIAN ART, Ananda K. Coomaraswamy. An unabridged republication of one of the finest books by a great scholar in Eastern art. Rich in descriptive material, history, social backgrounds; Sunga reliefs, Rajput paintings, Gupta temples, Burmese frescoes, textiles, jewelry, sculpture, etc. 400 photos. viii + 423pp. 6⅜ x 9¾.   21436-2 Paperbound $5.00

PRIMITIVE ART, Franz Boas. America's foremost anthropologist surveys textiles, ceramics, woodcarving, basketry, metalwork, etc.; patterns, technology, creation of symbols, style origins. All areas of world, but very full on Northwest Coast Indians. More than 350 illustrations of baskets, boxes, totem poles, weapons, etc. 378 pp.
                                        20025-6 Paperbound $3.00

THE GENTLEMAN AND CABINET MAKER'S DIRECTOR, Thomas Chippendale. Full reprint (third edition, 1762) of most influential furniture book of all time, by master cabinetmaker. 200 plates, illustrating chairs, sofas, mirrors, tables, cabinets, plus 24 photographs of surviving pieces. Biographical introduction by N. Bienenstock. vi + 249pp. 9⅞ x 12¾.   21601-2 Paperbound $4.00

AMERICAN ANTIQUE FURNITURE, Edgar G. Miller, Jr. The basic coverage of all American furniture before 1840. Individual chapters cover type of furniture— clocks, tables, sideboards, etc.—chronologically, with inexhaustible wealth of data. More than 2100 photographs, all identified, commented on. Essential to all early American collectors. Introduction by H. E. Keyes. vi + 1106pp. 7⅞ x 10¾.
                    21599-7, 21600-4 Two volumes, Paperbound $11.00

PENNSYLVANIA DUTCH AMERICAN FOLK ART, Henry J. Kauffman. 279 photos, 28 drawings of tulipware, Fraktur script, painted tinware, toys, flowered furniture, quilts, samplers, hex signs, house interiors, etc. Full descriptive text. Excellent for tourist, rewarding for designer, collector. Map. 146pp. 7⅞ x 10¾.
                                        21205-X Paperbound $2.50

EARLY NEW ENGLAND GRAVESTONE RUBBINGS, Edmund V. Gillon, Jr. 43 photographs, 226 carefully reproduced rubbings show heavily symbolic, sometimes macabre early gravestones, up to early 19th century. Remarkable early American primitive art, occasionally strikingly beautiful; always powerful. Text. xxvi + 207pp. 8⅜ x 11¼.   21380-3 Paperbound $3.50

ALPHABETS AND ORNAMENTS, Ernst Lehner. Well-known pictorial source for decorative alphabets, script examples, cartouches, frames, decorative title pages, calligraphic initials, borders, similar material. 14th to 19th century, mostly European. Useful in almost any graphic arts designing, varied styles. 750 illustrations. 256pp. 7 x 10. 21905-4 Paperbound $4.00

PAINTING: A CREATIVE APPROACH, Norman Colquhoun. For the beginner simple guide provides an instructive approach to painting: major stumbling blocks for beginner; overcoming them, technical points; paints and pigments; oil painting; watercolor and other media and color. New section on "plastic" paints. Glossary. Formerly *Paint Your Own Pictures*. 221pp. 22000-1 Paperbound $1.75

THE ENJOYMENT AND USE OF COLOR, Walter Sargent. Explanation of the relations between colors themselves and between colors in nature and art, including hundreds of little-known facts about color values, intensities, effects of high and low illumination, complementary colors. Many practical hints for painters, references to great masters. 7 color plates, 29 illustrations. x + 274pp. 20944-X Paperbound $2.75

THE NOTEBOOKS OF LEONARDO DA VINCI, compiled and edited by Jean Paul Richter. 1566 extracts from original manuscripts reveal the full range of Leonardo's versatile genius: all his writings on painting, sculpture, architecture, anatomy, astronomy, geography, topography, physiology, mining, music, etc., in both Italian and English, with 186 plates of manuscript pages and more than 500 additional drawings. Includes studies for the Last Supper, the lost Sforza monument, and other works. Total of xlvii + 866pp. 7⅞ x 10¾. 22572-0, 22573-9 Two volumes, Paperbound $10.00

MONTGOMERY WARD CATALOGUE OF 1895. Tea gowns, yards of flannel and pillow-case lace, stereoscopes, books of gospel hymns, the New Improved Singer Sewing Machine, side saddles, milk skimmers, straight-edged razors, high-button shoes, spittoons, and on and on . . . listing some 25,000 items, practically all illustrated. Essential to the shoppers of the 1890's, it is our truest record of the spirit of the period. Unaltered reprint of Issue No. 57, Spring and Summer 1895. Introduction by Boris Emmet. Innumerable illustrations. xiii + 624pp. 8½ x 11⅝. 22377-9 Paperbound $6.95

THE CRYSTAL PALACE EXHIBITION ILLUSTRATED CATALOGUE (LONDON, 1851). One of the wonders of the modern world—the Crystal Palace Exhibition in which all the nations of the civilized world exhibited their achievements in the arts and sciences—presented in an equally important illustrated catalogue. More than 1700 items pictured with accompanying text—ceramics, textiles, cast-iron work, carpets, pianos, sleds, razors, wall-papers, billiard tables, beehives, silverware and hundreds of other artifacts—represent the focal point of Victorian culture in the Western World. Probably the largest collection of Victorian decorative art ever assembled— indispensable for antiquarians and designers. Unabridged republication of the Art-Journal Catalogue of the Great Exhibition of 1851, with all terminal essays. New introduction by John Gloag, F.S.A. xxxiv + 426pp. 9 x 12. 22503-8 Paperbound $4.50

A History of Costume, Carl Köhler. Definitive history, based on surviving pieces of clothing primarily, and paintings, statues, etc. secondarily. Highly readable text, supplemented by 594 illustrations of costumes of the ancient Mediterranean peoples, Greece and Rome, the Teutonic prehistoric period; costumes of the Middle Ages, Renaissance, Baroque, 18th and 19th centuries. Clear, measured patterns are provided for many clothing articles. Approach is practical throughout. Enlarged by Emma von Sichart. 464pp.   21030-8 Paperbound $3.50

Oriental Rugs, Antique and Modern, Walter A. Hawley. A complete and authoritative treatise on the Oriental rug—where they are made, by whom and how, designs and symbols, characteristics in detail of the six major groups, how to distinguish them and how to buy them. Detailed technical data is provided on periods, weaves, warps, wefts, textures, sides, ends and knots, although no technical background is required for an understanding. 11 color plates, 80 halftones, 4 maps. vi + 320pp. 6⅛ x 9⅛.   22366-3 Paperbound $5.00

Ten Books on Architecture, Vitruvius. By any standards the most important book on architecture ever written. Early Roman discussion of aesthetics of building, construction methods, orders, sites, and every other aspect of architecture has inspired, instructed architecture for about 2,000 years. Stands behind Palladio, Michelangelo, Bramante, Wren, countless others. Definitive Morris H. Morgan translation. 68 illustrations. xii + 331pp.   20645-9 Paperbound $3.00

The Four Books of Architecture, Andrea Palladio. Translated into every major Western European language in the two centuries following its publication in 1570, this has been one of the most influential books in the history of architecture. Complete reprint of the 1738 Isaac Ware edition. New introduction by Adolf Placzek, Columbia Univ. 216 plates. xxii + 110pp. of text. 9½ x 12¾.
                     21308-0 Clothbound $10.00

Sticks and Stones: A Study of American Architecture and Civilization, Lewis Mumford.One of the great classics of American cultural history. American architecture from the medieval-inspired earliest forms to the early 20th century; evolution of structure and style, and reciprocal influences on environment. 21 photographic illustrations. 238pp.   20202-X Paperbound $2.00

The American Builder's Companion, Asher Benjamin. The most widely used early 19th century architectural style and source book, for colonial up into Greek Revival periods. Extensive development of geometry of carpentering, construction of sashes, frames, doors, stairs; plans and elevations of domestic and other buildings. Hundreds of thousands of houses were built according to this book, now invaluable to historians, architects, restorers, etc. 1827 edition. 59 plates. 114pp. 7⅞ x 10¾.
                     22236-5 Paperbound $3.50

Dutch Houses in the Hudson Valley Before 1776, Helen Wilkinson Reynolds. The standard survey of the Dutch colonial house and outbuildings, with constructional features, decoration, and local history associated with individual homesteads. Introduction by Franklin D. Roosevelt. Map. 150 illustrations. 469pp. 6⅝ x 9¼.   21469-9 Paperbound $4.00

THE ARCHITECTURE OF COUNTRY HOUSES, Andrew J. Downing. Together with Vaux's *Villas and Cottages* this is the basic book for Hudson River Gothic architecture of the middle Victorian period. Full, sound discussions of general aspects of housing, architecture, style, decoration, furnishing, together with scores of detailed house plans, illustrations of specific buildings, accompanied by full text. Perhaps the most influential single American architectural book. 1850 edition. Introduction by J. Stewart Johnson. 321 figures, 34 architectural designs. xvi + 560pp.
22003-6 Paperbound $4.00

LOST EXAMPLES OF COLONIAL ARCHITECTURE, John Mead Howells. Full-page photographs of buildings that have disappeared or been so altered as to be denatured, including many designed by major early American architects. 245 plates. xvii + 248pp. 7⅞ x 10¾. 21143-6 Paperbound $3.50

DOMESTIC ARCHITECTURE OF THE AMERICAN COLONIES AND OF THE EARLY REPUBLIC, Fiske Kimball. Foremost architect and restorer of Williamsburg and Monticello covers nearly 200 homes between 1620-1825. Architectural details, construction, style features, special fixtures, floor plans, etc. Generally considered finest work in its area. 219 illustrations of houses, doorways, windows, capital mantels. xx + 314pp. 7⅞ x 10¾. 21743-4 Paperbound $4.00

EARLY AMERICAN ROOMS: 1650-1858, edited by Russell Hawes Kettell. Tour of 12 rooms, each representative of a different era in American history and each furnished, decorated, designed and occupied in the style of the era. 72 plans and elevations, 8-page color section, etc., show fabrics, wall papers, arrangements, etc. Full descriptive text. xvii + 200pp. of text. 8⅜ x 11¼. 21633-0 Paperbound $5.00

THE FITZWILLIAM VIRGINAL BOOK, edited by J. Fuller Maitland and W. B. Squire. Full modern printing of famous early 17th-century ms. volume of 300 works by Morley, Byrd, Bull, Gibbons, etc. For piano or other modern keyboard instrument; easy to read format. xxxvi + 938pp. 8⅜ x 11. 21068-5, 21069-3 Two volumes, Paperbound $10.00

KEYBOARD MUSIC, Johann Sebastian Bach. Bach Gesellschaft edition. A rich selection of Bach's masterpieces for the harpsichord: the six English Suites, six French Suites, the six Partitas (Clavierübung part I), the Goldberg Variations (Clavierübung part IV), the fifteen Two-Part Inventions and the fifteen Three-Part Sinfonias. Clearly reproduced on large sheets with ample margins; eminently playable. vi + 312pp. 8⅛ x 11. 22360-4 Paperbound $5.00

THE MUSIC OF BACH: AN INTRODUCTION, Charles Sanford Terry. A fine, nontechnical introduction to Bach's music, both instrumental and vocal. Covers organ music, chamber music, passion music, other types. Analyzes themes, developments, innovations. x + 114pp. 21075-8 Paperbound $1.25

BEETHOVEN AND HIS NINE SYMPHONIES, Sir George Grove. Noted British musicologist provides best history, analysis, commentary on symphonies. Very thorough, rigorously accurate; necessary to both advanced student and amateur music lover. 436 musical passages. vii + 407 pp. 20334-4 Paperbound $2.75

JOHANN SEBASTIAN BACH, Philipp Spitta. One of the great classics of musicology, this definitive analysis of Bach's music (and life) has never been surpassed. Lucid, nontechnical analyses of hundreds of pieces (30 pages devoted to St. Matthew Passion, 26 to B Minor Mass). Also includes major analysis of 18th-century music. 450 musical examples. 40-page musical supplement. Total of xx + 1799pp.

(EUK) 22278-0, 22279-9 Two volumes, Clothbound $17.50

MOZART AND HIS PIANO CONCERTOS, Cuthbert Girdlestone. The only full-length study of an important area of Mozart's creativity. Provides detailed analyses of all 23 concertos, traces inspirational sources. 417 musical examples. Second edition. 509pp. 21271-8 Paperbound $3.50

THE PERFECT WAGNERITE: A COMMENTARY ON THE NIBLUNG'S RING, George Bernard Shaw. Brilliant and still relevant criticism in remarkable essays on Wagner's Ring cycle, Shaw's ideas on political and social ideology behind the plots, role of Leitmotifs, vocal requisites, etc. Prefaces. xxi + 136pp.

(USO) 21707-8 Paperbound $1.50

DON GIOVANNI, W. A. Mozart. Complete libretto, modern English translation; biographies of composer and librettist; accounts of early performances and critical reaction. Lavishly illustrated. All the material you need to understand and appreciate this great work. Dover Opera Guide and Libretto Series; translated and introduced by Ellen Bleiler. 92 illustrations. 209pp.

21134-7 Paperbound $2.00

HIGH FIDELITY SYSTEMS: A LAYMAN'S GUIDE, Roy F. Allison. All the basic information you need for setting up your own audio system: high fidelity and stereo record players, tape records, F.M. Connections, adjusting tone arm, cartridge, checking needle alignment, positioning speakers, phasing speakers, adjusting hums, trouble-shooting, maintenance, and similar topics. Enlarged 1965 edition. More than 50 charts, diagrams, photos. iv + 91pp. 21514-8 Paperbound $1.25

REPRODUCTION OF SOUND, Edgar Villchur. Thorough coverage for laymen of high fidelity systems, reproducing systems in general, needles, amplifiers, preamps, loudspeakers, feedback, explaining physical background. "A rare talent for making technicalities vividly comprehensible," R. Darrell, *High Fidelity*. 69 figures. iv + 92pp. 21515-6 Paperbound $1.25

HEAR ME TALKIN' TO YA: THE STORY OF JAZZ AS TOLD BY THE MEN WHO MADE IT, Nat Shapiro and Nat Hentoff. Louis Armstrong, Fats Waller, Jo Jones, Clarence Williams, Billy Holiday, Duke Ellington, Jelly Roll Morton and dozens of other jazz greats tell how it was in Chicago's South Side, New Orleans, depression Harlem and the modern West Coast as jazz was born and grew. xvi + 429pp.

21726-4 Paperbound $2.50

FABLES OF AESOP, translated by Sir Roger L'Estrange. A reproduction of the very rare 1931 Paris edition; a selection of the most interesting fables, together with 50 imaginative drawings by Alexander Calder. v + 128pp. 6½x9¼.

21780-9 Paperbound $1.50

AGAINST THE GRAIN (A REBOURS), Joris K. Huysmans. Filled with weird images, evidences of a bizarre imagination, exotic experiments with hallucinatory drugs, rich tastes and smells and the diversions of its sybarite hero Duc Jean des Esseintes, this classic novel pushed 19th-century literary decadence to its limits. Full unabridged edition. Do not confuse this with abridged editions generally sold. Introduction by Havelock Ellis. xlix + 206pp. 22190-3 Paperbound $2.00

VARIORUM SHAKESPEARE: HAMLET. Edited by Horace H. Furness; a landmark of American scholarship. Exhaustive footnotes and appendices treat all doubtful words and phrases, as well as suggested critical emendations throughout the play's history. First volume contains editor's own text, collated with all Quartos and Folios. Second volume contains full first Quarto, translations of Shakespeare's sources (Belleforest, and Saxo Grammaticus), Der Bestrafte Brudermord, and many essays on critical and historical points of interest by major authorities of past and present. Includes details of staging and costuming over the years. By far the best edition available for serious students of Shakespeare. Total of xx + 905pp. 21004-9, 21005-7, 2 volumes, Paperbound $7.00

A LIFE OF WILLIAM SHAKESPEARE, Sir Sidney Lee. This is the standard life of Shakespeare, summarizing everything known about Shakespeare and his plays. Incredibly rich in material, broad in coverage, clear and judicious, it has served thousands as the best introduction to Shakespeare. 1931 edition. 9 plates. xxix + 792pp. (USO) 21967-4 Paperbound $3.75

MASTERS OF THE DRAMA, John Gassner. Most comprehensive history of the drama in print, covering every tradition from Greeks to modern Europe and America, including India, Far East, etc. Covers more than 800 dramatists, 2000 plays, with biographical material, plot summaries, theatre history, criticism, etc. "Best of its kind in English," New Republic. 77 illustrations. xxii + 890pp. 20100-7 Clothbound $8.50

THE EVOLUTION OF THE ENGLISH LANGUAGE, George McKnight. The growth of English, from the 14th century to the present. Unusual, non-technical account presents basic information in very interesting form: sound shifts, change in grammar and syntax, vocabulary growth, similar topics. Abundantly illustrated with quotations. Formerly Modern English in the Making. xii + 590pp. 21932-1 Paperbound $3.50

AN ETYMOLOGICAL DICTIONARY OF MODERN ENGLISH, Ernest Weekley. Fullest, richest work of its sort, by foremost British lexicographer. Detailed word histories, including many colloquial and archaic words; extensive quotations. Do not confuse this with the Concise Etymological Dictionary, which is much abridged. Total of xxvii + 830pp. 6½ x 9¼. 21873-2, 21874-0 Two volumes, Paperbound $6.00

FLATLAND: A ROMANCE OF MANY DIMENSIONS, E. A. Abbott. Classic of science-fiction explores ramifications of life in a two-dimensional world, and what happens when a three-dimensional being intrudes. Amusing reading, but also useful as introduction to thought about hyperspace. Introduction by Banesh Hoffmann. 16 illustrations. xx + 103pp. 20001-9 Paperbound $1.00

POEMS OF ANNE BRADSTREET, edited with an introduction by Robert Hutchinson. A new selection of poems by America's first poet and perhaps the first significant woman poet in the English language. 48 poems display her development in works of considerable variety—love poems, domestic poems, religious meditations, formal elegies, "quaternions," etc. Notes, bibliography. viii + 222pp.

22160-1 Paperbound $2.50

THREE GOTHIC NOVELS: THE CASTLE OF OTRANTO BY HORACE WALPOLE; VATHEK BY WILLIAM BECKFORD; THE VAMPYRE BY JOHN POLIDORI, WITH FRAGMENT OF A NOVEL BY LORD BYRON, edited by E. F. Bleiler. The first Gothic novel, by Walpole; the finest Oriental tale in English, by Beckford; powerful Romantic supernatural story in versions by Polidori and Byron. All extremely important in history of literature; all still exciting, packed with supernatural thrills, ghosts, haunted castles, magic, etc. xl + 291pp.

21232-7 Paperbound $2.50

THE BEST TALES OF HOFFMANN, E. T. A. Hoffmann. 10 of Hoffmann's most important stories, in modern re-editings of standard translations: Nutcracker and the King of Mice, Signor Formica, Automata, The Sandman, Rath Krespel, The Golden Flowerpot, Master Martin the Cooper, The Mines of Falun, The King's Betrothed, A New Year's Eve Adventure. 7 illustrations by Hoffmann. Edited by E. F. Bleiler. xxxix + 419pp.

21793-0 Paperbound $3.00

GHOST AND HORROR STORIES OF AMBROSE BIERCE, Ambrose Bierce. 23 strikingly modern stories of the horrors latent in the human mind: The Eyes of the Panther, The Damned Thing, An Occurrence at Owl Creek Bridge, An Inhabitant of Carcosa, etc., plus the dream-essay, Visions of the Night. Edited by E. F. Bleiler. xxii + 199pp.

20767-6 Paperbound $1.50

BEST GHOST STORIES OF J. S. LEFANU, J. Sheridan LeFanu. Finest stories by Victorian master often considered greatest supernatural writer of all. Carmilla, Green Tea, The Haunted Baronet, The Familiar, and 12 others. Most never before available in the U. S. A. Edited by E. F. Bleiler. 8 illustrations from Victorian publications. xvii + 467pp.

20415-4 Paperbound $3.00

MATHEMATICAL FOUNDATIONS OF INFORMATION THEORY, A. I. Khinchin. Comprehensive introduction to work of Shannon, McMillan, Feinstein and Khinchin, placing these investigations on a rigorous mathematical basis. Covers entropy concept in probability theory, uniqueness theorem, Shannon's inequality, ergodic sources, the E property, martingale concept, noise, Feinstein's fundamental lemma, Shanon's first and second theorems. Translated by R. A. Silverman and M. D. Friedman. iii + 120pp.

60434-9 Paperbound $1.75

SEVEN SCIENCE FICTION NOVELS, H. G. Wells. The standard collection of the great novels. Complete, unabridged. *First Men in the Moon, Island of Dr. Moreau, War of the Worlds, Food of the Gods, Invisible Man, Time Machine, In the Days of the Comet.* Not only science fiction fans, but every educated person owes it to himself to read these novels. 1015pp. (USO) 20264-X Clothbound $5.00

LAST AND FIRST MEN AND STAR MAKER, TWO SCIENCE FICTION NOVELS, Olaf Stapledon. Greatest future histories in science fiction. In the first, human intelligence is the "hero," through strange paths of evolution, interplanetary invasions, incredible technologies, near extinctions and reemergences. Star Maker describes the quest of a band of star rovers for intelligence itself, through time and space: weird inhuman civilizations, crustacean minds, symbiotic worlds, etc. Complete, unabridged. v + 438pp. (USO) 21962-3 Paperbound $2.50

THREE PROPHETIC NOVELS, H. G. WELLS. Stages of a consistently planned future for mankind. *When the Sleeper Wakes,* and *A Story of the Days to Come,* anticipate *Brave New World* and *1984,* in the 21st Century; *The Time Machine,* only complete version in print, shows farther future and the end of mankind. All show Wells's greatest gifts as storyteller and novelist. Edited by E. F. Bleiler. x + 335pp. (USO) 20605-X Paperbound $2.50

THE DEVIL'S DICTIONARY, Ambrose Bierce. America's own Oscar Wilde— Ambrose Bierce—offers his barbed iconoclastic wisdom in over 1,000 definitions hailed by H. L. Mencken as "some of the most gorgeous witticisms in the English language." 145pp. 20487-1 Paperbound $1.25

MAX AND MORITZ, Wilhelm Busch. Great children's classic, father of comic strip, of two bad boys, Max and Moritz. Also Ker and Plunk (Plisch und Plumm), Cat and Mouse, Deceitful Henry, Ice-Peter, The Boy and the Pipe, and five other pieces. Original German, with English translation. Edited by H. Arthur Klein; translations by various hands and H. Arthur Klein. vi + 216pp.
20181-3 Paperbound $2.00

PIGS IS PIGS AND OTHER FAVORITES, Ellis Parker Butler. The title story is one of the best humor short stories, as Mike Flannery obfuscates biology and English. Also included, That Pup of Murchison's, The Great American Pie Company, and Perkins of Portland. 14 illustrations. v + 109pp. 21532-6 Paperbound $1.25

THE PETERKIN PAPERS, Lucretia P. Hale. It takes genius to be as stupidly mad as the Peterkins, as they decide to become wise, celebrate the "Fourth," keep a cow, and otherwise strain the resources of the Lady from Philadelphia. Basic book of American humor. 153 illustrations. 219pp. 20794-3 Paperbound $1.50

PERRAULT'S FAIRY TALES, translated by A. E. Johnson and S. R. Littlewood, with 34 full-page illustrations by Gustave Doré. All the original Perrault stories— Cinderella, Sleeping Beauty, Bluebeard, Little Red Riding Hood, Puss in Boots, Tom Thumb, etc.—with their witty verse morals and the magnificent illustrations of Doré. One of the five or six great books of European fairy tales. viii + 117pp. 8⅛ x 11. 22311-6 Paperbound $2.00

OLD HUNGARIAN FAIRY TALES, Baroness Orczy. Favorites translated and adapted by author of the *Scarlet Pimpernel.* Eight fairy tales include "The Suitors of Princess Fire-Fly," "The Twin Hunchbacks," "Mr. Cuttlefish's Love Story," and "The Enchanted Cat." This little volume of magic and adventure will captivate children as it has for generations. 90 drawings by Montagu Barstow. 96pp.
22293-4 Paperbound $1.95

THE RED FAIRY BOOK, Andrew Lang. Lang's color fairy books have long been children's favorites. This volume includes Rapunzel, Jack and the Bean-stalk and 35 other stories, familiar and unfamiliar. 4 plates, 93 illustrations x + 367pp.
21673-X Paperbound $2.50

THE BLUE FAIRY BOOK, Andrew Lang. Lang's tales come from all countries and all times. Here are 37 tales from Grimm, the Arabian Nights, Greek Mythology, and other fascinating sources. 8 plates, 130 illustrations. xi + 390pp.
21437-0 Paperbound $2.50

HOUSEHOLD STORIES BY THE BROTHERS GRIMM. Classic English-language edition of the well-known tales — Rumpelstiltskin, Snow White, Hansel and Gretel, The Twelve Brothers, Faithful John, Rapunzel, Tom Thumb (52 stories in all). Translated into simple, straightforward English by Lucy Crane. Ornamented with headpieces, vignettes, elaborate decorative initials and a dozen full-page illustrations by Walter Crane. x + 269pp.
21080-4 Paperbound $2.00

THE MERRY ADVENTURES OF ROBIN HOOD, Howard Pyle. The finest modern versions of the traditional ballads and tales about the great English outlaw. Howard Pyle's complete prose version, with every word, every illustration of the first edition. Do not confuse this facsimile of the original (1883) with modern editions that change text or illustrations. 23 plates plus many page decorations. xxii + 296pp.
22043-5 Paperbound $2.50

THE STORY OF KING ARTHUR AND HIS KNIGHTS, Howard Pyle. The finest children's version of the life of King Arthur; brilliantly retold by Pyle, with 48 of his most imaginative illustrations. xviii + 313pp. 6⅛ x 9¼.
21445-1 Paperbound $2.50

THE WONDERFUL WIZARD OF OZ, L. Frank Baum. America's finest children's book in facsimile of first edition with all Denslow illustrations in full color. The edition a child should have. Introduction by Martin Gardner. 23 color plates, scores of drawings. iv + 267pp.
20691-2 Paperbound $2.50

THE MARVELOUS LAND OF OZ, L. Frank Baum. The second Oz book, every bit as imaginative as the Wizard. The hero is a boy named Tip, but the Scarecrow and the Tin Woodman are back, as is the Oz magic. 16 color plates, 120 drawings by John R. Neill. 287pp.
20692-0 Paperbound $2.50

THE MAGICAL MONARCH OF MO, L. Frank Baum. Remarkable adventures in a land even stranger than Oz. The best of Baum's books not in the Oz series. 15 color plates and dozens of drawings by Frank Verbeck. xviii + 237pp.
21892-9 Paperbound $2.25

THE BAD CHILD'S BOOK OF BEASTS, MORE BEASTS FOR WORSE CHILDREN, A MORAL ALPHABET, Hilaire Belloc. Three complete humor classics in one volume. Be kind to the frog, and do not call him names . . . and 28 other whimsical animals. Familiar favorites and some not so well known. Illustrated by Basil Blackwell. 156pp.
(USO) 20749-8 Paperbound $1.50

EAST O' THE SUN AND WEST O' THE MOON, George W. Dasent. Considered the best of all translations of these Norwegian folk tales, this collection has been enjoyed by generations of children (and folklorists too). Includes True and Untrue, Why the Sea is Salt, East O' the Sun and West O' the Moon, Why the Bear is Stumpy-Tailed, Boots and the Troll, The Cock and the Hen, Rich Peter the Pedlar, and 52 more. The only edition with all 59 tales. 77 illustrations by Erik Werenskiold and Theodor Kittelsen. xv + 418pp. 22521-6 Paperbound $3.50

GOOPS AND HOW TO BE THEM, Gelett Burgess. Classic of tongue-in-cheek humor, masquerading as etiquette book. 87 verses, twice as many cartoons, show mischievous Goops as they demonstrate to children virtues of table manners, neatness, courtesy, etc. Favorite for generations. viii + 88pp. 6½ x 9¼. 22233-0 Paperbound $1.25

ALICE'S ADVENTURES UNDER GROUND, Lewis Carroll. The first version, quite different from the final Alice in Wonderland, printed out by Carroll himself with his own illustrations. Complete facsimile of the "million dollar" manuscript Carroll gave to Alice Liddell in 1864. Introduction by Martin Gardner. viii + 96pp. Title and dedication pages in color. 21482-6 Paperbound $1.25

THE BROWNIES, THEIR BOOK, Palmer Cox. Small as mice, cunning as foxes, exuberant and full of mischief, the Brownies go to the zoo, toy shop, seashore, circus, etc., in 24 verse adventures and 266 illustrations. Long a favorite, since their first appearance in St. Nicholas Magazine. xi + 144pp. 6⅝ x 9¼. 21265-3 Paperbound $1.75

SONGS OF CHILDHOOD, Walter De La Mare. Published (under the pseudonym Walter Ramal) when De La Mare was only 29, this charming collection has long been a favorite children's book. A facsimile of the first edition in paper, the 47 poems capture the simplicity of the nursery rhyme and the ballad, including such lyrics as I Met Eve, Tartary, The Silver Penny. vii + 106pp. (USO) 21972-0 Paperbound $1.25

THE COMPLETE NONSENSE OF EDWARD LEAR, Edward Lear. The finest 19th-century humorist-cartoonist in full: all nonsense limericks, zany alphabets, Owl and Pussycat, songs, nonsense botany, and more than 500 illustrations by Lear himself. Edited by Holbrook Jackson. xxix + 287pp. (USO) 20167-8 Paperbound $2.00

BILLY WHISKERS: THE AUTOBIOGRAPHY OF A GOAT, Frances Trego Montgomery. A favorite of children since the early 20th century, here are the escapades of that rambunctious, irresistible and mischievous goat—Billy Whiskers. Much in the spirit of Peck's Bad Boy, this is a book that children never tire of reading or hearing. All the original familiar illustrations by W. H. Fry are included: 6 color plates, 18 black and white drawings. 159pp. 22345-0 Paperbound $2.00

MOTHER GOOSE MELODIES. Faithful republication of the fabulously rare Munroe and Francis "copyright 1833" Boston edition—the most important Mother Goose collection, usually referred to as the "original." Familiar rhymes plus many rare ones, with wonderful old woodcut illustrations. Edited by E. F. Bleiler. 128pp. 4½ x 6⅜. 22577-1 Paperbound $1.00

Two Little Savages; Being the Adventures of Two Boys Who Lived as Indians and What They Learned, Ernest Thompson Seton. Great classic of nature and boyhood provides a vast range of woodlore in most palatable form, a genuinely entertaining story. Two farm boys build a teepee in woods and live in it for a month, working out Indian solutions to living problems, star lore, birds and animals, plants, etc. 293 illustrations. vii + 286pp.
20985-7 Paperbound $2.50

Peter Piper's Practical Principles of Plain & Perfect Pronunciation. Alliterative jingles and tongue-twisters of surprising charm, that made their first appearance in America about 1830. Republished in full with the spirited woodcut illustrations from this earliest American edition. 32pp. 4½ x 6⅜.
22560-7 Paperbound $1.00

Science Experiments and Amusements for Children, Charles Vivian. 73 easy experiments, requiring only materials found at home or easily available, such as candles, coins, steel wool, etc.; illustrate basic phenomena like vacuum, simple chemical reaction, etc. All safe. Modern, well-planned. Formerly *Science Games for Children*. 102 photos, numerous drawings. 96pp. 6⅛ x 9¼.
21856-2 Paperbound $1.25

An Introduction to Chess Moves and Tactics Simply Explained, Leonard Barden. Informal intermediate introduction, quite strong in explaining reasons for moves. Covers basic material, tactics, important openings, traps, positional play in middle game, end game. Attempts to isolate patterns and recurrent configurations. Formerly *Chess*. 58 figures. 102pp. (USO) 21210-6 Paperbound $1.25

Lasker's Manual of Chess, Dr. Emanuel Lasker. Lasker was not only one of the five great World Champions, he was also one of the ablest expositors, theorists, and analysts. In many ways, his Manual, permeated with his philosophy of battle, filled with keen insights, is one of the greatest works ever written on chess. Filled with analyzed games by the great players. A single-volume library that will profit almost any chess player, beginner or master. 308 diagrams. xli x 349pp.
20640-8 Paperbound $2.75

The Master Book of Mathematical Recreations, Fred Schuh. In opinion of many the finest work ever prepared on mathematical puzzles, stunts, recreations; exhaustively thorough explanations of mathematics involved, analysis of effects, citation of puzzles and games. Mathematics involved is elementary. Translated by F. Göbel. 194 figures. xxiv + 430pp. 22134-2 Paperbound $3.00

Mathematics, Magic and Mystery, Martin Gardner. Puzzle editor for Scientific American explains mathematics behind various mystifying tricks: card tricks, stage "mind reading," coin and match tricks, counting out games, geometric dissections, etc. Probability sets, theory of numbers clearly explained. Also provides more than 400 tricks, guaranteed to work, that you can do. 135 illustrations. xii + 176pp.
20335-2 Paperbound $1.50

MATHEMATICAL PUZZLES FOR BEGINNERS AND ENTHUSIASTS, Geoffrey Mott-Smith. 189 puzzles from easy to difficult—involving arithmetic, logic, algebra, properties of digits, probability, etc.—for enjoyment and mental stimulus. Explanation of mathematical principles behind the puzzles. 135 illustrations. viii + 248pp.
20198-8 Paperbound $1.75

PAPER FOLDING FOR BEGINNERS, William D. Murray and Francis J. Rigney. Easiest book on the market, clearest instructions on making interesting, beautiful origami. Sail boats, cups, roosters, frogs that move legs, bonbon boxes, standing birds, etc. 40 projects; more than 275 diagrams and photographs. 94pp.
20713-7 Paperbound $1.00

TRICKS AND GAMES ON THE POOL TABLE, Fred Herrmann. 79 tricks and games— some solitaires, some for two or more players, some competitive games—to entertain you between formal games. Mystifying shots and throws, unusual caroms, tricks involving such props as cork, coins, a hat, etc. Formerly *Fun on the Pool Table*. 77 figures. 95pp.
21814-7 Paperbound $1.00

HAND SHADOWS TO BE THROWN UPON THE WALL: A SERIES OF NOVEL AND AMUSING FIGURES FORMED BY THE HAND, Henry Bursill. Delightful picturebook from great-grandfather's day shows how to make 18 different hand shadows: a bird that flies, duck that quacks, dog that wags his tail, camel, goose, deer, boy, turtle, etc. Only book of its sort. vi + 33pp. 6½ x 9¼. 21779-5 Paperbound $1.00

WHITTLING AND WOODCARVING, E. J. Tangerman. 18th printing of best book on market. "If you can cut a potato you can carve" toys and puzzles, chains, chessmen, caricatures, masks, frames, woodcut blocks, surface patterns, much more. Information on tools, woods, techniques. Also goes into serious wood sculpture from Middle Ages to present, East and West. 464 photos, figures. x + 293pp.
20965-2 Paperbound $2.00

HISTORY OF PHILOSOPHY, Julián Marias. Possibly the clearest, most easily followed, best planned, most useful one-volume history of philosophy on the market; neither skimpy nor overfull. Full details on system of every major philosopher and dozens of less important thinkers from pre-Socratics up to Existentialism and later. Strong on many European figures usually omitted. Has gone through dozens of editions in Europe. 1966 edition, translated by Stanley Appelbaum and Clarence Strowbridge. xviii + 505pp. 21739-6 Paperbound $3.50

YOGA: A SCIENTIFIC EVALUATION, Kovoor T. Behanan. Scientific but non-technical study of physiological results of yoga exercises; done under auspices of Yale U. Relations to Indian thought, to psychoanalysis, etc. 16 photos. xxiii + 270pp.
20505-3 Paperbound $2.50

Prices subject to change without notice.
Available at your book dealer or write for free catalogue to Dept. GI, Dover Publications, Inc., 180 Varick St., N. Y., N. Y. 10014. Dover publishes more than 150 books each year on science, elementary and advanced mathematics, biology, music, art, literary history, social sciences and other areas.